SATAN'S BIG FAT LIE

STEVE FOSS

SATAN's BIG FAT LIE

 CHARISMA HOUSE

Visit the author's website at www.stevefoss.com.

Cataloging-in-Publication Data is on file with the Library of Congress.
International Standard Book Number: 978-1-63641-122-4
E-book ISBN: 978-1-63641-123-1

While the author has made every effort to provide accurate internet addresses at the time of publication, neither the publisher nor the author assumes any responsibility for errors or for changes that occur after publication. Further, the publisher does not have any control over and does not assume any responsibility for author or third-party websites or their content.

22 23 24 25 26 — 9 8 7 6 5 4 3 2 1
Printed in the United States of America

CONTENTS

FOREWORD

FOR SEVENTY YEARS I have had the honor of being an ordained minister in full-time ministry as a pastor, evangelist, missionary, and owner of a Christian television station. I met Steve Foss in 1987 in San Diego when he was a dynamic teenage born-again Christian, and I added him to our ministry team as a youth leader to begin a campus ministry at a local high school.

This campus outreach grew and was soon citywide, with many teens coming to Christ through the ministry. Steve's anointed preaching and healing ministry have since expanded to reach many thousands throughout the world.

We now live in the last days, and many are unaware that a great amount of our turmoil comes from being invaded by demonic powers, what Scripture calls "spiritual hosts of wickedness in the heavenly places" (Eph. 6:12). As a minister of the gospel of Jesus Christ with a proven record of knowing the leading of the Holy Spirit and speaking forcefully to timely issues, Steve is an instrument of God's delivering power for this generation.

"To everything there is a season, a time for every purpose under heaven" (Eccles. 3:1). The Bible and world history also indicate that there is a man or woman chosen to lead "every purpose." Many voices express viewpoints with very few results—in fact, many times those voices only add to the turmoil. In *Satan's Big Fat Lie,* Steve shares a biblical perspective, his personal victories, and verified testimonies of others to give a "straight from the heart" plan for winning!

—JERRY BARNARD
PASTOR, HORIZON CHURCH
DAYTONA BEACH, FLORIDA

INTRODUCTION

As I have traveled the nations of the world for more than thirty years, I have seen a consistent, devastating, highly effective weapon used by Satan to defeat, discourage, and destroy Christians. This weapon has caused great turmoil in many people's lives. It was the first fruit of the fall of man in the Garden of Eden, and it was the final enemy Jesus had to defeat to fulfill His destiny upon the cross.

Over the last twenty years the Lord has taken me into several prophetic visions and dreams to expose the working of this strategy of the enemy and how to overcome it. The first chapter of *Satan's Big Fat Lie* describes an amazing vision of the intense spiritual battles coming before the return of Christ. It reveals what is going on within the church and how the enemy discourages, defeats, and damages God's people.

Most Christians have suffered loss, setbacks, and failures.

Some have even walked away from God as a result, being filled with confusion, disappointment, and deep hurts.

Many Christians battle deep feelings of failure, insecurity, and self-judgment, thinking they will never measure up. We are beaten down by the constant assault of accusations from the world, social media, cultural shifts, and even from some fellow Christians.

The assaults upon the Christian faith by the media, government and educational institutions, businesses, and even false doctrines coming from the pulpit have caused many to question where the Lord is. They're wondering when the promises of God will be fulfilled and whether the prophecies being declared in many churches are just hype.

This book will take you deep into the spirit realm to unveil Satan's big fat lie. You will clearly see how he uses one particular weapon to wear you out spiritually and make you want to quit. You will discover the amazing realms of victory and strength that God has for you and how to boldly stand up to the onslaught against Jesus, His church, and the Word of God.

As I have preached this message around the world, I have never seen such a positive reaction. Pastors and leaders have begged me to preach it wherever I go. I have watched leaders fall on their faces in tears as God sets them free. I have seen tears streaming down people's faces as they feel the love and freedom Christ has made available for them. Never in more than thirty years of ministry have I seen a message have such an impact upon people's lives. Many pastors have said this is the most important message for God's people in these days.

If you have been falsely accused, this book is for you.

If you have failed publicly in any area of your life, this book is for you.

If you have been mocked by friends and family for daring to believe God and His Word, this book is for you.

If you have gone through a divorce, experienced the pain of a loved one trapped by addiction, or been ostracized by the church and/or the world, this book is for you.

If you have been belittled or suffered from abuse, bullying, rejection, racism, or judgment, this book is for you.

If you have felt the pressure to stop standing for holiness and righteousness, this book is for you.

Multitudes around the world have been empowered and strengthened by my previous best-selling book, *Satan's Dirty Little Secret*. Now *Satan's Big Fat Lie* will take you to the next incredible level and give you the strategies to defeat Satan's greatest weapon. My prayer is that through this book God will give you the power to stand strong and free and be filled with joy and hope in the midst of the chaos of our present world.

PART I

THE BATTLE
WE ALL FACE

CHAPTER 1

THE VISION

IN THE SPRING of 2000 I was leading worship during a prayer meeting at the church I was pastoring when I was suddenly standing on a large battlefield. On one side was the army of God led by Jesus. On the other was a long single row of demons. Both armies stretched as far as the eye could see.

The army of God was fully clothed in magnificent white armor, and the soldiers were standing at attention, each in perfect order and arrayed for battle. Jesus was front and center of the army, sitting on a beautiful, majestic white horse. I had never seen a horse so magnificent. Its strength, muscle tone, size, and bright white hair were glorious to behold.

Behind the army were huge military-style tanks about two stories tall. The guns on the front of the tanks were also huge, about two feet in diameter. Each of the tanks had one of the gifts of the Spirit written on its side: faith, words of wisdom, words of knowledge, tongues, interpretation of tongues, gifts of healing, working of miracles, prophecy, and discerning of spirits.

Far behind the army of God and the tanks was a wall of billowing fire and smoke that rose from the ground all the way to the sky. At this point I knew I was seeing the final end-time judgment of God.

As I looked on the other side of the battlefield I saw terror on the demons' faces. They weren't running away, but they had a look of impending doom. Their weapons were tattered and old—a collection of single-shot muskets, bows and arrows, and rusty swords. Compared with the powerful-looking weapons of the army of God, these old weapons looked feeble, but they could still cause injury and death.

Behind this single row of demons I saw various encampments. There were hundreds or even thousands of them. In the middle of each encampment was a flagpole with a banner flying overhead. The banners had the name of the main demonic stronghold over that particular camp. Some read "pride"; others, "hatred, murder, bitterness, sexual perversion, lust, fear, delusion, greed, distraction, revelries, slumber," or "worship of demons." Even though many demonic spirits were at work in each camp, it seemed there was always a main ruling spirit from which all the other demons were being empowered.

The camps were surrounded by demons that acted like guards. The guards formed a circle around the camp, yet in each camp there was always a large gap through which anyone could have easily walked out. However, the prisoners had such poor eyesight that they seemed not to be aware of the gaps.

Inside each camp I saw sickly people. Some were shuffling around as though they walked with a limp, others were crawling, and many others lay unable to move. There were small fires throughout the camps that many of these prisoners would gather around. Although the fires provided a small amount of light, they produced no heat. Even so the prisoners would gather close to the fires and stretch out their hands as if to warm themselves. They seemed unaware that the fires produced no heat.

The camps were all dark and dingy. The ground was covered with human dung, and it was hot, steamy, smelly, and acidic. A thick cloud covered the land, and there was a perpetual darkness.

Most of the prisoners were either blind or could see no more than a couple of feet in front of them. The stronger prisoners who could still wander around, although with a limp, also had poor eyesight. I watched them walk near the gaps in the lines of guards, yet none ever left these prison camps.

I asked the Lord, "Who are these prisoners, and what are these camps?" The Lord said, "These camps are cities, and the prisoners are My churches." Upon hearing this I was heartbroken and shocked at how weak, blind, and diseased the churches were.

As I watched the prisoners I saw that many would reach down to the ground and eat some of the dung. When they ate the dung, they would stand up a bit stronger and taller for a few moments, but then they would quickly become weaker and more diseased. I asked the Lord, "What is this dung?" He said, "It is the works of the flesh. Many of My people in these camps think the dung is the work of My Spirit. They eat the dung thinking they are eating of the freedom of My Spirit and that they are doing the work of My kingdom."

Boils and festering wounds covered many of them. The wounds oozed a smelly pus that dripped off them onto the dung-covered ground.

I was shocked by how diseased, weak, and bound the prisoners were. "These are God's churches?" I thought to myself. As I looked at the fires I noticed that some of the stronger prisoners who could wander around would occasionally try to join with the prisoners hovering around a fire. Often the ones around the fire would attempt to drive the newcomers away. They were afraid of the other prisoners and thought they had come to steal from them.

I also saw some of the people gathered around these fires occasionally become aware of other nearby fires. If they tried to explore the other fires, other prisoners around them would try to stop them. They would tell them the other fires were false fires and of the devil. "We have the real fire, and you must stay here," they would say. They would even get violent and beat fellow prisoners who tried to leave their fire.

I looked in amazement as the Lord revealed to me that these fires represented truths that these individual groups had discovered. These truths did produce a small amount of light but not enough by themselves to illuminate the reality of the prison camps or the gaps in the lines of guards they could escape through. The prisoners were so afraid of losing their fires that they fought anyone trying to leave their fire to explore other fires and were very suspicious of any other prisoners (churches) who wanted to join their little group around their fire.

Depression was a major issue I noticed in every

camp—depression and a lack of spiritual sight, which resulted in great fear. The majority of the prisoners seemed to be in a survival mode. They were just trying to hold on and completely unaware of their condition.

The next thing I knew I was back with the army of God. As we began to march the enemy shot their muskets and arrows. Some members of God's army took off pieces of their armor as they were marching. It seemed they did this because the battle was long and they didn't want to carry all that weight. They seemed to believe they could be safe and do fine without certain pieces of the armor. As soon as they would let down the armor, even slightly, the arrows or shots of the enemy would hit them.

As rusty and old as the enemy's weapons were, I was surprised by how accurate the demons' aim was. Once any part of the Lord's soldiers was exposed because they lowered their armor, almost immediately the enemy's shots would hit them in the exposed areas. When this happened the soldier would become weaker. If the soldier didn't repent and put the armor back on, they would become weaker and weaker. The soldier would also, in their weariness, start taking off more pieces of the armor because now it seemed too heavy, and eventually the soldier fell to the ground. I knew if those soldiers didn't get up they would be consumed by the final judgment.

As the army marched toward the enemy's front line, the tanks began to fire. Two or three of the tanks would fire in unison at a particular camp. Faith and healing would fire together, or tongues and interpretation, or maybe prophecy with the working of miracles and healing. As the projectiles flew from the tanks they would explode over the city. The gifts of the Spirit released by the tanks would destroy the banners over the city, and the demons would begin to flee. However, the prisoners still wouldn't leave the camps. They continued to wander around as before, unable to perceive what was happening. It wasn't until God's army arrived at the camps that the prisoners responded.

When God's army hit the enemy's front line it collapsed immediately. It was amazing how powerless the demons were before the fully armed saints. As the Lord's army arrived at the various camps, the brightness of their white garments would cause the prisoners' eyes to open.

Every prisoner was shocked by who was in the army of God. These prisoners (churches) had been in darkness for so long that when they saw the true, victorious saints they all declared in shock, "It's you?" Then about half of them gave the soldiers a huge smile and reached out their hands to them. When they did this they were immediately lifted up, healed, and cleansed, and their garments became white.

But when the other half of the prisoners saw who the true army of God was, they turned away in disgust, saying, "Not you!" After the prisoners who rejected the true army of God turned back, they lay down in the dung and quickly became more diseased than before. I knew at this point that they had rejected the truth and the Lord Himself and would end up being consumed by the wall of fire and judgment. Then the vision ended.

TWO ADDITIONS TO THE VISION

The vision continued in two main experiences, each ten years apart. In 2010, while in my prayer room, I was suddenly taken back into the vision. The great battle for the cities and the churches was behind us, and now the much larger, glorious army of God was coming to a massive battlefield. This time the enemy's forces also were larger. I saw row after row of demons, dozens deep and extending as far as my eye could see. Behind the horde of hell was the mass of lost humanity.

At the head of the Lord's army, in the center of a massive line, stood Jesus, looking straight ahead. He never flinched or turned to the side. No matter what happened He was focused on something far ahead.

We stayed still for a season on the battlefield, as if to gather ourselves and take in the scope of the battle ahead. Then Jesus took His sword and stretched it in front of Him. What looked like lightning shot out of the tip of His sword and expanded, covering the entire width of the enemy's battle lines.

I heard myself shouting along with the Lord's army. It was exhilarating, and I thought, "This is it. With one shot Jesus has destroyed all the enemy's forces." Or so I thought. The tanks began to fire again but more rapidly, like machine guns. This was an end-time release of the gifts of the Spirit unlike anything ever seen before.

To my surprise, though, the demons didn't flee. They dropped their weapons and reached behind them and filled slingshots with softball-sized piles of hot, steamy dung. It was like what I had seen previously in the camps but even more vile. The demons began to fling the dung at the entire army of God. Everyone got hit. Not a single person was spared.

Some just got nicked on a toe or hand, some got hit on an arm or leg, others got full hits to the chest or shoulders, and others even got hit full on their faces. The dung was like acid and immediately began to eat through whatever it hit.

All the members of the army tried to wipe it off. Some used their hands, others their shields or swords. But no matter what they used, the dung would only spread to the thing they tried to use to get it off them. The dung would spread and grow. I felt a sense of concern from those who got hit on the toe or hand and a sense of panic from those who got hit on the face or chest.

It seemed that nothing we were doing would help. Watching this scene, I cried out to Jesus and said, "Lord, what do we do?" Jesus said, "Look unto Me." When we looked at Jesus, a bright, white light exploded from His body, and we were all instantly cleansed and restored. But the soldiers who didn't look to Jesus but stayed focused on trying to get rid of the dung were quickly overcome.

I asked the Lord, "What was this dung attack?" He said, "In the last days the enemy is going to unleash a massive attack of the works of the flesh such as has never been seen before. Nobody will escape being hit by this attack. Only those who keep their eyes fixed on Me will be able to overcome this assault of wickedness."

Then roughly ten years later, in 2021, I was taken back into this vision exactly where the previous one had left off. The army began marching forward. The demons continued to unleash volley after volley of dung upon the army of God. The closer we got to the enemy's battle lines, the faster and more intense were the attacks of the works of the flesh.

I saw many more soldiers falling away. They would get their eyes off Jesus and be overcome by the dung as it spread all over their bodies until they were consumed and fell to the ground. They would then become so covered with dung that they looked as if they had been buried in a shallow grave.

I looked at Jesus as this was happening, and He never flinched or looked back. His focus was straight ahead. I thought He was focused on the massive sea of lost humanity, but then I realized He was looking past them. I wondered in my heart what Jesus was looking at.

Then I heard a voice say, "He is focused on the end of the age." I then saw beyond the sea of lost humanity, and there appeared a huge, empty white throne. The thought filled my mind, "Why is it empty? Where is the Father?" I then realized this was Jesus' throne to rule and reign from here on the earth.

I glanced back toward the fallen soldiers and wondered why Jesus wasn't stopping to take care of them. I could feel a hidden presence in the rear of the fallen soldiers and sensed that the Lord had a plan but wasn't going to stop for anything until the end of the age.

I could make out what looked like an angel standing over each fallen soldier in a shallow grave. As the army marched forward into the unrelenting assault of the enemy, explosion after explosion of the white, purifying light kept cleansing and restoring the army. The moment they got hit they would look to Jesus and instantly be cleansed and restored.

It looked to me that each time the soldiers got hit and cleansed, they actually got stronger. The unrelenting assault of the enemy was producing the opposite of what the demons wanted on the soldiers who kept their eyes on Jesus. The more those soldiers got hit the more powerful they became. Instead of causing them to get weary, the intensity of the battle actually strengthened them.

When God's army arrived at the front line of the enemy, all the soldiers drew their swords, but they did so while keeping their right arms straight down at their sides. They just rotated their wrists to extend their swords straight in front of them. The soldiers did this simultaneously and with great force. The sound of them drawing their swords and shifting into position was so loud I literally jumped while I was seeing this vision.

As soon as the tip of the sword touched a demon that spirit would immediately flee. It was like the way oil on the surface of water dispels when it's hit with soap. Desperation filled the enemy's ranks, and the demons began to panic. In the panic many demons began to run toward the sea of lost humanity. They would grab people by the head and slit their throats. They wanted to kill as many as they could before these lost souls could surrender to Jesus.

As this horrific scene played out, I realized something. Usually the devil is more interested in getting people to yield to him than in killing them because his power only increases on the earth as he has willing vessels who yield themselves to his wickedness. But at the end of the age he will know his time is short, and he will change his main strategy to simply killing as many people as possible to keep them from coming to Christ.

While this slaughter was happening I also saw many from the sea of lost humanity suddenly become spirit beings and be translated from the enemy's side to the army of the Lord. I was then carried back to the field where the fallen soldiers were buried. They weren't dead;

they were trapped under the dung. The angels over each soldier were looking with deep care at them and seemed to be protecting them. You could feel the love and concern coming from these angels. It also seemed they were waiting for something to happen.

Then a gentle, cool wind began to blow from behind the battlefield. The breeze cooled and dried out the dung. The wind was so clean and refreshing. It was gentle yet also carried great power. The dung, once dried, simply blew away and uncovered the fallen soldiers.

As the soldiers were revealed, they began to move and rise up out of the shallow graves. Their skin was still covered with dirt, but the remnants of dung were no longer acidic. As I watched several rise up I noticed they were a bit disoriented, like someone coming out of a deep sleep.

As they rose they all started to look for Jesus. All of them had trouble seeing at first. Some had blurry vision; others couldn't see at all. I heard cries. Some said, "Jesus is so far away." Others couldn't see Jesus at all and cried, "He left me. How could He leave me?"

Jesus had continued to move forward in the battle and was now quite a distance away from where these soldiers had fallen. The angels encouraged them, "Just look to Jesus; He's closer than you think. Ask for eye salve." The soldiers were still covered with a dark coating. It was the darkness of shame. This was going to be a great battle for some to overcome.

Some responded quickly and asked the Lord for eye salve so they could see. When they asked for the salve, a clear, thick substance the size of a small egg appeared in their angels' hands, and the angels applied it to the soldiers' eyes. Then suddenly they could see. Their countenance lit up, and the darkness fled from them as they began to shine bright white.

Others panicked and said, "I'm lost, I'm lost! I can't see." The angels had great patience and care for these fallen soldiers. The angels told the rising soldiers, "You must pick up your armor and present it back to the Lord so He can cleanse it."

That statement seemed odd to me, and I questioned it in my heart. "Each piece of the armor is a revelation of the Word and truth," I thought, "so why would it need to be cleansed?" A voice spoke to me and said, "The reason they fell is because a lie got mixed in with the truth they once walked in. The lie made them vulnerable and weakened them. They must submit the armor back to the Lord so He can remove the perversions and purify what they believe. Truth will protect you, but a little lie produces deception. Deception is a great tool of the enemy at the end of the age."

I then saw crows flying down, attacking these rising soldiers and trying to pluck out their eyes. The screeching of the crows pierced through me, but it wasn't just noise. They were screaming, "Shame! Shame!" They would land on the soldiers' shoulders, scream in their ears, "Shame! Shame," and try to pluck out their eyes.

The angels, who were mostly very calm and patient, yelled at the soldiers, saying, "Pick up your sword and pick up your helmet. The helmet has an eye shield, and it protects your vision. It will keep your focus on Jesus and His mission."

The angels could not chase the crows away; only the soldiers could do that. The angels could only instruct the soldiers what to do. If the soldiers simply picked up the sword, the crows would fly off their shoulders, though the crows would still cry, "Shame! Shame," and continue trying to pluck out their eyes.

I then focused on one soldier who had crows on his shoulders. He picked up his sword and put on his helmet. As the sword and helmet were presented to the Lord, they began to glow bright white. The helmet was the helmet of the hope of salvation.

As the soldier tried to look to Jesus, the crows kept screaming, "Shame! Shame!" The soldier then looked down at himself and saw the filth he had been buried in, and he began to feel very weak. He just stood there dwelling on what had happened to him.

The angel said, "Focus on Jesus and what He is focused on. You must get back into the battle. You must start marching. As you do this the helmet will cancel the noise of the crows." The soldier did what the angel told him. As he focused on Jesus and what Jesus was focused on, which was the end of the age, the screaming of the crows and the noise of the battle quickly began to fade.

The more he focused on Jesus and the end of the age, the quieter things got. The soldier then clearly heard the still, small voice of the Lord.

"Pick up the rest of your armor and follow Me closely," Jesus said, "for I have restored your faith and gifted you with new insight. As you march forward, you will see other buried soldiers. I want you to care for them, cover them, and protect them. Pray for the wind of My Spirit to blow away the dung. You are to be unto them as My angels. Instruct them as the others instructed you. You will restore many who have fallen."

The soldier cried out, "But Lord, I want to be a part of the frontline battle for the harvest."

Jesus said, "You will, but you must also be My angel of restoration for those who have fallen. You now have the compassion they need to be healed. This is the gift I have given to you because you have overcome."

The soldier looked puzzled. "Overcome?" he said. "Lord, I took my eyes off You so much that I became buried in the works of the flesh and lay as one dead to You. How can You say I have overcome?"

"Son," Jesus said, "that's shame speaking to you again, for you look at your lowest point and judge your success on that. But I look to the fact that you came back to Me and looked unto Me. Peter denied Me three times, yet I said to Peter before he denied Me, 'I have prayed for you, that your faith should not fail; and when you have returned to Me, strengthen your brethren' [Luke 22:32]. Those who have failed Me the greatest and have returned I entrust with the mandate to strengthen others who are facing what you have faced."

Then I looked out over the battlefield where the fallen soldiers were awakening. I saw what looked like swarms of crows (not flocks, as they acted more like swarms of locusts). I wondered why I hadn't seen them like this before.

Then a voice spoke to me and said, "Because of your shame. Shame hides in darkness. It is hard to see because it causes its victims to look at themselves. When your eyes are on yourself and not on Me, you will not be able to see that it is the enemy who is attacking you. Shame has always been one of Satan's most powerful and effective weapons. It often cloaks itself in the guise of self-awareness. It is the result of eating of the tree of the knowledge of good and evil.

"Shame will always set your eyes on yourself and keep

you from being able to rightly discern Me or My will. When Adam ate of the tree in the garden, he couldn't see Me as the God of restoration but only as the God of judgment. That is why he hid from Me. He was afraid of My righteous judgment.

"Adam and Eve immediately became filled with shame when they ate of the tree. They tried to cover themselves. When I came calling, they were afraid and tried to hide themselves from Me. Adam heard Me as I came in the Spirit of the day. I came to him as I do to all whom I love. I came to expose the sin and bring them back to Me.

"But having eaten of the fruit, Adam became filled with shame. He saw his nakedness. He was now more focused on his shame than on Me. He was now in a self-preservation mode. Run, hide, cover, accuse, blame—he would do anything he could do to deal with the shame.

"The first words out of My mouth were to expose the shame. I said, 'Who told you that you were naked?' I wanted to expose to Adam that the internal voice of shame was not his voice but the voice of another."

Then I heard the angel that was helping the fallen soldier say, "It was the voice of the crows that Adam and Eve heard." He continued, "The crows are black and impossible to see in the darkness. Only in the light of the knowledge of the glory of God, as revealed in the face of Jesus, can you see them.

"You will always walk in darkness when your eyes are on yourself. Shame will always lead you to blame others and then eventually God. Shame causes deep hurt. It produces a painful feeling. The other soldiers you saw were immediately attacked with shame as they began to rise from their graves. This is why they reacted with so much hurt when they realized Jesus had continued to pursue His mission in proceeding to the end of the age. Shame told them Jesus had left them behind, but this was not true."

"I will never leave you nor forsake you," another voice said. I turned and looked to see who was speaking. As I turned to face the rear of the battlefield, I felt a gentle, cool wind blowing. I saw no one, and I couldn't tell where the voice and the wind were coming from.

The wind was so refreshing, as it was filled with life. I just stood there for a moment, closed my eyes, and allowed the gentle wind of refreshing to blow on and through me. I stood there so still, taking slow, deep breaths. Everything became calm and quiet. Instead of the dark, dirty, smelly, death-filled battlefield, my mind and senses became filled with this beauty.

It seemed I was now standing in a beautiful meadow. As I focused on the wind, I found myself feeling like I was being transported to another place. I was aware that I was in the battlefield, but my mind, my spirit, my emotions, and even my senses were becoming overwhelmed with the beauty of this meadow.

I could smell the flowers and hear the bubbling of a little brook as I felt the warmth of a beautiful spring day. A stillness and calm washed over and through me. I just waited there not saying anything. I just stood still, basking in the experience.

My mind was so peaceful; not one thought passed through my mind. It was a moment of perfect peace. Then I heard the voice again.

"I am the wind of the Spirit; I am the breath of life; I am the seasons of refreshing from the presence of the Lord.

"I am the renewer of strength. I am perfect peace.

"I am joy unspeakable and full of glory. I am the river of living water. I am the fountain. I am the restorer of streets to dwell in. I am the hope of glory.

"I have always been and always will be. I am the Spirit of truth. I am the unity of the Spirit. I am the manifestation of the Three.

"I am the Holy Spirit."

Then I said, "I don't see You." It was so weird because it seemed as if I could see a smile in my mind's eye.

The Spirit said, "I am like the wind. I am everywhere, ever changing, always moving. In the midst of the storms and battles in the days ahead, I have reserved this place for you. It is a place of perfect peace, a place of refreshing and renewal. My people in these last days will learn to walk in this place while also in the battle. I am their refuge; I am their dwelling place."

When I opened my eyes, I was still standing in the battlefield, yet the sense of perfect peace was now abiding in me. I then heard the voice of the Spirit say, "You can learn to dwell here, but you must keep your eyes on Jesus and off yourself. The battle is raging, and the enemy has unleashed his great end-time plan. You must go and warn My people of the strategy of the enemy. Warn them of the impending onslaught of the works of the flesh and the battle of shame. I have given you a gift to bring restoration to My fallen soldiers. I have anointed you to bring them deliverance from the torment of shame by bringing them truth.

"There is much more I will yet show you about the battle ahead and the end of the age, but now you must go and bring this message to My people. Warn them, equip them, deliver them, and empower them. Teach them to come to

My secret place. Teach them to dwell with Me in perfect peace. Teach them to focus on Jesus and the end of the age. Teach them that they can and must walk free from shame."

⌒⚮⚮

Throughout this book I will often refer back to this vision and to another supernatural experience I will share in chapter 4, as there are many incredible spiritual insights in both of the experiences. I believe God wants to use these revelations to show you that no matter what you have done, what failures you may have endured, or what others have done around or to you, as a born-again believer you do not have to put on the garment of shame.

Shame is something none of us can avoid; every one of us must fight against it. It is a great enemy that had the potential to cause even Jesus to give up on His mission. Shame was the final, massive attack Satan threw at Jesus to get Him to come down off the cross, and he uses the same tactic against us. In the pages that follow I will show you what the Lord has revealed to me about overcoming shame. Together we will discover how to rise up, pick up our weapons of warfare, and break the curse of shame.

CHAPTER 2

JESUS' BATTLE WITH SHAME

Jesus was tempted and tested in all points, just as we are. Hebrews 4:15 tells us, "We do not have a High Priest who cannot sympathize with our weaknesses, but was in all points tempted as we are, yet without sin." Jesus suffered what we suffer and showed us how to overcome.

The enemy repeatedly used the mighty weapon of shame against Jesus. It was his final assault against Jesus to get Him to quit and not fulfill His destiny.

One of the most profound portions of Scripture is found in Hebrews 12.

> Therefore we also, since we are surrounded by so great a cloud of witnesses, let us lay aside every weight, and the sin which so easily ensnares us, and let us run with endurance the race that is set before us, looking unto Jesus, the author and finisher of our faith, who for the joy that was set before Him endured the cross, despising the shame, and has sat down at the right hand of the throne of God. For consider Him who endured such hostility from sinners against Himself, lest you become weary and discouraged in your souls.
>
> —Hebrews 12:1–3

The writer of Hebrews tells us to "lay aside every weight, and the sin which so easily ensnares us" (12:1). The Word of God always explains itself. As a result I am always asking God questions. When I looked at this verse I noticed two issues. The first was these weights and the second was the sin, both of which so easily ensnare us.

The Greek word translated "ensnares" is *euperistatos*. It means to control tightly, constricting, obstructing, easily distracting.[1] The sense of the word is the ability to skillfully encircle on all sides to attack, assail, or hinder action.[2]

Hebrews 12:1 instructs us to run with endurance. The sense of the word *endurance* is to have the power—especially the inward fortitude—necessary to withstand hardships or stress. The implication here about these weights and sin is that they so easily encircle us on all sides and attack, assail, and hinder us from having the inward fortitude and power to withstand the hardships and stresses we face in living a life of faith.

It is easy for most of us to acknowledge by experience that unconfessed, unrepented sin can easily surround and rob us of our inward strength. When sin is active in our lives we quickly become spiritually weary and often quit pressing in to Christ with all our heart, mind, soul, and strength.

The fact is that sin will suck the life out of you. There are some extreme teachings on grace surging through the body of Christ that basically say once you're saved, sin is no longer an issue. They say stop trying to manage sin; stop worrying about it; you're forgiven, so it doesn't really matter how you live.

If you try to live that way, after a while you will find out that sin will so easily ensnare you. It will encircle and entrap you, and the enemy will use that sin stronghold in your life to further assail and suck the life out of you. Sin kills.

Consider the following verses, which are talking to Christians.

> But those who desire to be rich fall into temptation and a snare, and into many foolish and harmful lusts which drown men in destruction and perdition. For the love of money is a root of all kinds of evil, for which some have strayed from the faith in their greediness, and pierced themselves through with many sorrows.
>
> —1 TIMOTHY 6:9–10

> But each one is tempted when he is drawn away by his own desires and enticed. Then, when desire has conceived, it gives birth to sin; and sin, when it is full-grown, brings forth death.
>
> —JAMES 1:14–15

Unrepented sin will ensnare you. But thanks be to God, we have an advocate with the Father.

We can easily understand how sin ensnares us, but what are these weights? I believe the writer of Hebrews points us directly at the answer: "looking unto Jesus, the author and finisher of our faith, who for the joy that was set before Him endured the cross, *despising the shame*" (Heb. 12:2, emphasis added).

Nothing is accidentally placed in Scripture. The one thing in the middle of the battle at the cross was shame. Shame was the great, final weapon Satan used against Jesus to try to rob Him of the power to endure the suffering of the cross.

Try to imagine the emotional experience of crucifixion from Jesus' perspective. Jesus is "the only begotten Son, who is in the bosom of the Father" (John 1:18). He has beheld the glory of His Father and prayed, "And now, O Father, glorify Me together with Yourself, with the glory which I had with You before the world was" (John 17:5). Jesus "is the image of the invisible God, the firstborn over all creation" (Col. 1:15); "in Him is no darkness at all" (1 John 1:5); and "in Him was life, and the life was the light of men" (John 1:4).

"The Son of Man did not come to be served, but to serve, and to give His life a ransom for many" (Mark 10:45). He "made Himself of no reputation, taking the form of a bondservant, and coming in the likeness of men" (Phil. 2:7). And He said, "I have come that they may have life, and that they may have it more abundantly. I am the good shepherd. The good shepherd gives His life for the sheep" (John 10:10–11).

As Jesus was entering Jerusalem a few days prior to dying on the cross, "a very great multitude spread their clothes on the road; others cut down branches from the trees and spread them on the road. Then the multitudes who went before and those who followed cried out, saying: 'Hosanna to the Son of David! 'Blessed is He who comes in the name of the Lord!' Hosanna in the highest!" (Matt. 21:8–9).

Now, after being so celebrated, after all the miracles, after all the sacrifice, after living a sinless life for the glory of God, Jesus was going to experience shame to its fullest degree. It began in the Garden of Gethsemane. Jesus had just spent hours in travailing prayer, to the point where drops of blood came out of His pores. Then "he who was called Judas, one of the twelve, went before them and drew near to Jesus to kiss Him. But Jesus said to him, 'Judas, are you betraying the Son of Man with a kiss?'" (Luke 22:47–48).

Shame comes in many forms from many sources. There is shame when someone you love betrays you. Judas came with a multitude to fulfill the prophecy in Psalm 69:19: "You know my reproach, my shame, and my dishonor; my adversaries are all before You."

Then "having arrested Him, they led Him and brought Him into the high priest's house" (Luke 22:54). Peter followed at a distance, and after some time while Jesus was being interrogated, Peter was repeatedly asked if he was with Jesus. Finally, someone said, "'Surely you are one of them; for you are a Galilean, and your speech shows it.' Then he [Peter] began to curse and swear, 'I do not know this Man of whom you speak!'" (Mark 14:70–71). And, apparently being in earshot, "the Lord turned and looked at Peter" (Luke 22:61).

We so often focus on Peter weeping bitterly, but what about Jesus? In His hour of greatest need, even His closest companions ran from Him and denied Him. Scripture says, "Then all the disciples forsook Him and fled" (Matt. 26:56).

Shame was assaulting our Lord. "Shame on You," the enemy said. "All Your friends—those whom You gave so much to—have forsaken You. They couldn't even stay awake while You prayed. They have run for their lives. You are all alone. Shame on You, Jesus; shame on You!"

Jesus experienced what we experience. Again, Hebrews 4:15 says, "For we do not have a High Priest who cannot sympathize with our weaknesses, but was in all points tempted as we are, yet without sin."

We read that "the men who held Jesus mocked Him and beat Him. And having blindfolded Him, they struck Him on the face and asked Him, saying, 'Prophesy! Who is the one who struck You?' And many other things they blasphemously spoke against Him" (Luke 22:63–65). And the voice of the enemy spoke even louder, saying, "Shame on You, Jesus; shame on You! You're nothing; You're weak; You're deceived; You're a failure. Everybody has left You; nobody believes You. You're a disgrace to Judaism. Shame on You, Jesus. Shame on You!"

I can imagine the enemy throwing the temptation in the wilderness back in His face: "He shall give His angels charge over you, to keep you...in their hands they shall bear you up, lest you dash your foot against a stone" (Luke 4:10–11). As one who has experienced the tormenting voice of the accuser, I must believe that Satan was throwing all he had at Jesus. The devil was leaving nothing on the table.

JESUS WAS MOCKED AND ATTACKED WITH SHAME

After Jesus was brought before Pilate the first time, He was sent to King Herod.

> Then he questioned Him with many words, but He answered him nothing. And the chief priests and scribes stood and vehemently accused Him. Then Herod, with his men of war, treated Him with contempt and mocked Him, arrayed Him in a gorgeous robe, and sent Him back to Pilate. That very day Pilate and Herod became friends with each other, for previously they had been at enmity with each other.
> —LUKE 23:9–12

They treated Jesus with contempt and mocked Him, and the enemy's voice continued to get louder and louder. You will find that in seasons when the enemy is attacking you through shame, even people who previously didn't like each other will join forces to assail you. Pilate and Herod became friends as they united in persecuting Jesus under this demonic spirit of shame.

They brought Jesus back before Pilate, and when Pilate said he found no guilt in Jesus and wanted to release Him, the crowd, being stirred up by leaders operating under a religious spirit, demanded that Jesus be crucified. Just a few days earlier the people were singing His praises, prophetically declaring Him to be a king. Now they were demanding He be killed in the cruelest, most hideous manner in that day: crucifixion. Jesus was going to die like a murderer, thief, or traitor. The enemy's voice was still speaking, "Shame on You, Jesus. Shame on You!"

The shame, torture, and suffering continued.

> So Pilate, wanting to gratify the crowd, released Barabbas to them; and he delivered Jesus, after he had scourged Him, to be crucified.
>
> Then the soldiers led Him away into the hall called Praetorium, and they called together the whole garrison. And they clothed Him with purple; and they twisted a crown of thorns, put it on His head [Shame on You, Jesus; shame on You!], and began to salute Him, "Hail, King of the Jews!" [Shame on You, Jesus!] Then they struck Him on the head with a reed and spat on Him [Shame on You, Jesus!]; and bowing the knee, they worshiped Him. And when they had mocked Him, they took the purple off Him, put His own clothes on Him, and led Him out to crucify Him.
>
> —MARK 15:15–20

Shame was assaulting Jesus at every step of the process. The textbook definition of shame is: "a painful feeling of humiliation or distress caused by the consciousness of wrong or foolish behavior"; "a loss of respect or esteem; dishonor"; "a person, action, or situation that brings a loss of respect or honor."[3]

Only the most hideous criminals were taken outside the city to be killed. Imagine yourself in Jesus' place. Imagine the shame and humiliation He felt after having given so much and loved people so much. The multitudes had followed Him and worshipped Him, and then just a few days later He was being led out of the city as the worst of criminals and paraded before the people, who knew only the vilest offenders deserved this form of public humiliation and death. "Shame on You, Jesus; shame on You!" the tormenting spirits yelled.

Jesus was taken to Calvary, stripped naked, and nailed to the cross, all while the crowd was cheering and the guards were mocking Him, "saying, 'He saved others; let Him save Himself if He is the Christ, the chosen of God.' The soldiers also mocked Him, coming and offering Him sour wine, and saying, 'If You are the King of the Jews, save Yourself.'...Then one of the criminals who were hanged blasphemed Him, saying, 'If You are the Christ, save Yourself and us'" (Luke 23:35–37, 39). The voices were screaming: "If You are the Christ, if You are the Christ, if You are the Christ....You're not who You claim to be. Shame on You. You're a blasphemer of God. Shame on You. Prove Yourself. Shame on You."

Jesus had told His disciples, "Do you think that I cannot now pray to My Father, and He will provide Me with more than twelve legions of angels?" (Matt. 26:53). Yet despite this He "endured the cross, despising the shame" (Heb. 12:2).

With all the shame He was enduring through false accusations, public humiliation, being made a spectacle—stripped, tortured, brutalized—and rejected by the very people He came to save, Jesus was about to face His greatest battle with shame yet. Jesus was about to experience the shame of sin. God "made Him who knew no sin to be sin for us" (2 Cor. 5:21). All the sin of every person to ever live flooded inside Christ as Scripture says, "And the Lord has laid on Him the iniquity of us all" (Isa. 53:6).

The sin of every liar, cheater, adulterer, murderer, rapist, pedophile, sexual pervert, blasphemer, Satan worshipper, lover of evil, and hater of God was flooding the perfect, sinless Son of God. Now Jesus was experiencing the vileness of the sins of all humanity. He was experiencing the shame of actual sin.

Overwhelmed by this reality, He looked up to His Father for help and strength, and He experienced the ultimate shame. He who had been one with the Father from before the beginning was now looking to see the Father's loving eyes on Him in His greatest hour of need, but the Father could not look upon Him. The Father had to turn His gaze from Jesus because He cannot look upon sin. The oneness, the fellowship, the eternal divine connection was broken. Surely Jesus must have heard the enemy saying, "Shame on You, Jesus. All the shame is on You!"

Crying out with a pain deeper than that of a mother who just lost her only child, He screamed, "My God, My God, why have You forsaken Me?" (Mark 15:34). Then He took His last breath.

He was despised and rejected—a man of sorrows, acquainted with deepest grief. We turned our backs on him and looked the other way. He was despised, and we did not care. Yet it was our weaknesses he carried; it was our sorrows that weighed him down. And we thought his troubles were a punishment from God, a punishment for his own sins! But he was pierced for our rebellion, crushed for our sins. He was beaten so we could be whole. He was whipped so we could be healed. All of us, like sheep, have strayed away. We have left God's paths to follow our own.

Yet the Lord laid on him the sins of us all. He was oppressed and treated harshly, yet he never said a word. He was led like a lamb to the slaughter. And as a sheep is silent before the shearers, he did not open his mouth. Unjustly condemned, he was led away. No one cared that he died without descendants, that his life was cut short in midstream. But he was struck down for the rebellion of my people. He had done no wrong and had never deceived anyone. But he was buried like a criminal; he was put in a rich man's grave.

But it was the Lord's good plan to crush him and cause him grief. Yet when his life is made an offering for sin, he will have many descendants. He will enjoy a long life, and the Lord's good plan will prosper in his hands. When he sees all that is accomplished by his anguish, he will be satisfied. And because of his experience, my righteous servant will make it possible for many to be counted righteous, for he will bear all their sins. I will give him the honors of a victorious soldier, because he exposed himself to death. He was counted among

the rebels. He bore the sins of many and interceded
for rebels.

—Isaiah 53:3–12, nlt

Jesus bore our sin and shame. Again, He "was in all points tempted as we are, yet without sin. Let us therefore come boldly to the throne of grace, that we may obtain mercy and find grace to help in time of need" (Heb. 4:15–16). Jesus was not only tempted to sin; He was tempted to yield to the lie of shame. He was only able to endure the suffering of the cross because He learned to despise the shame.

But how? How did Jesus keep from falling for Satan's big fat lie? How did He learn to break the curse of shame? Let's journey on together, back to the Garden of Eden, to discover how you and I can do what Jesus did.

CHAPTER 3

WHERE IT ALL BEGAN

S HAME WAS THE final enemy Jesus had to defeat to endure the cross and fulfill His mission of paying the price for the sins of the world and conquering death, hell, and the grave. However, shame was also the very first manifestation of the fruit of sin in the Garden of Eden.

Now the serpent was more cunning than any beast of the field which the Lord God had made. And he said to the woman, "Has God indeed said, 'You shall not eat of every tree of the garden'?" And the woman said to the serpent, "We may eat the fruit of the trees of the garden; but of the fruit of the tree which is in the midst of the garden, God has said, 'You shall not eat it, nor shall you touch it, lest you die.'"

Then the serpent said to the woman, "You will not surely die. For God knows that in the day you eat of it your eyes will be opened, and you will be like God, knowing good and evil." So when the woman saw that the tree was good for food, that

it was pleasant to the eyes, and a tree desirable to
make one wise, she took of its fruit and ate. She also
gave to her husband with her, and he ate.
—GENESIS 3:1–6

In my book *Satan's Dirty Little Secret*, I expose Satan's
strategy in the garden and the two demon spirits he
released upon Eve. This great deception that came upon
Eve led her to disobey God and eat the fruit of the tree of
the knowledge of good and evil.

She then gave of the fruit to Adam, and he also ate
in disobedience to God. Then a horrific thing took
place. Suddenly something had changed.
Then the eyes of both of them were opened, and
they knew that they were naked; and they sewed fig
leaves together and made themselves coverings.
—GENESIS 3:7

The Bible says their eyes were opened and they knew
they were naked. Many have speculated as to what this
means. Some believe they were covered in God's glory, and
when they sinned that glory departed from them. This
concept has basis in Scripture as we will see later; however,
let's first focus on the fact that they became aware they
were naked. Why was this such a revelation to them, and
why did they react so quickly to it?

The answer can be found in Genesis 2:25: "And they were
both naked, the man and his wife, and were *not ashamed*"
(emphasis added). Adam and Eve were naked the whole
time. The verse clearly says they were naked, but they lacked
any shame. However, immediately after their disobedience,
the first manifestation of the fruit of their sin was that they

became ashamed. The focus on the nakedness is to draw our attention to the fact that now Adam and Eve were not only fully self-aware but also filled with shame.

God had told them, "But the tree of the knowledge of good and evil you shall not eat, for in the day that you eat of it you shall surely die" (Gen. 2:17). We know they did not immediately die physically, but the death process was released into humankind. Death was now at work in mankind, and its very first manifestation was shame.

Put this deep into your spirit: shame was the very first thing mankind had to deal with as a result of sin, and shame was the very last thing Jesus had to overcome when paying the price of our sins. The spirit of shame was released upon Adam and Eve and ultimately upon all mankind.

The word translated "ashamed" in Genesis 2:25 is *bôš*, which means "to have a painful feeling and emotional distress (sometimes to the point of despair) by having done something wrong, with an associative meaning of having the disapproval of those around them....Note: This wrong can refer to a social mistake, or a serious sin."[1]

Shame is a devastating and debilitating weapon Satan has used against mankind to dominate and manipulate us in hopes of driving us further and further from God. Adam and Eve immediately tried to cover their shame, but to no avail. They grabbed some fig leaves and covered themselves, but when they heard the voice of the Lord they still ran and hid. None of our human efforts can remove our shame; only the revelation of Jesus Christ can.

We all have experienced this. We all have sinned and then felt the conviction of the presence and Word of the Lord. Having pastored youth for many years, I learned to recognize when people were struggling. One week they would be up front in the front rows worshipping, praying, and deeply engaged in the service. Then the next week they would drag in late and sit in the back row. They would try to put on a good face, but I could see there was a distance. It never took long to discover they had sinned and were ashamed.

When they felt like they were doing well spiritually, they were boldly going before the throne of grace. But when they felt they had messed up, they were hesitant and withdrawn, having lost a sense of confidence in God's love for them. One week they were asking God for citywide revival, and the next they were asking God just to help them. They went from praying for the sick to standing back in the shadows when the altar ministry was happening. Shame can drive even the most committed Christians out of church and away from God.

We all have experienced it. When you feel like you are spiritually "on"—when you feel like you're doing well and have the victory—you have confidence, boldness, faith, joy, and so much more. When you are dealing with the spirit of shame, you become fearful, withdrawn, angry, sad, miserable, and self-focused, and you tend to blame others for your situation.

Shame will always cause you to focus on yourself and not God. The pain of shame is real and tormenting. This is why mankind will grab for anything to cover and remove their shame.

The need to be free from shame is so powerful it has opened a door for many false prophets and teachers to lead people to reject the sound doctrine of a life of continual confession and repentance of sin, brokenness before God, and pursuit of holiness and replace it with a false message of grace that removes all consequences of sin and any need to repent and stop sinning. These false teachers say that once you're saved, you never need to be concerned about sin because Christians don't sin. If there is no sin, then there is no guilt and condemnation; in other words, there is no shame.

I deal extensively with the hyper-grace message and how destructive it is to understanding the true power of grace in my book *Grace Is Not a Get Out of Hell Free Card.* The hyper-grace message that is being embraced by much of the church today cannot and will not protect you from the powerful spirit of shame sweeping the world.

The fact is, the hyper-grace message doesn't work. Just as the fig leaves didn't remove Adam and Eve's shame, simply pretending that God doesn't see your sin and there is no need for repentance once you're saved will never remove the death process and power of shame. Shame will drive you away from God. It will drive you away from His presence, away from the truth of His Word, and away from the cross you must carry to be His disciple.

Adam tried to find a way of covering his shame without facing God and what he had done. He grabbed fig leaves. There is various speculation as to what kind of tree the tree of the knowledge of good and evil was. The Bible is not clear on this, but some believe it was a fig tree because Adam and Eve immediately grabbed fig leaves and sewed them together to cover their nakedness.

As the Lord was unveiling the truth about breaking the curse of shame to me, I began to ask Him questions, the main one being, "Why fig leaves?" I discovered two main reasons Adam and Eve grabbed fig leaves.

First they grabbed the fig leaves to try to cover their

shame. This is something mankind is always looking for ways to do. We try to cover our shame by denying our sin, passing blame for our sin, rejecting God's moral law, making excuses, lying, deceiving, hiding, self-medicating, intellectualizing, hardening our hearts, and even rewriting history. But no matter how clever, creative, or intense our efforts are, mankind cannot ever truly cover our own shame. Only the blood of Jesus can remove our shame.

I discovered the second main reason Adam and Eve grabbed fig leaves while studying the history of the fig leaf in ancient times. The fig leaf has a sap on it that causes many people to develop a painful rash. I thought, "Why would Adam and Eve place upon the most delicate parts of their bodies a leaf that could cause a painful rash?" Is it possible they knew this would happen? Is it possible they wanted to punish themselves for their sin?

So often and in so many ways we try to pay a price for our sin to alleviate the shame. We try to make up for it by doing good deeds. We try to inflict pain on ourselves by verbally beating ourselves up. We accept and embrace public shaming because we believe we deserve it.

Adam and Eve's covering their most sensitive parts with a leaf that causes a painful rash may very well be the first act of penance. But there is only One who could ever pay the price for our sin—only One who was perfect and thus able to be a substitute for us upon the cross. Only Jesus, through the shedding of His blood, could ever pay for our sin and shame.

JESUS AND THE FIG TREE

I was recently talking with a man who has been on many archeological digs in Israel. He was sharing with me about the discovery several years back of the Pool of Siloam in Jerusalem, which was found when the steps that led up to the ancient temple were unearthed.[2] Under the steps was the Gihon, spoken of in Genesis 2 as one of four rivers that flowed out of the Garden of Eden (vv. 10–14).

I know many have thought the Gihon of Eden and the Gihon in Jerusalem were two different waterways, but experts I've spoken with and trust now believe they are one and the same. This is why some scholars believe the Garden of Eden was actually located in present-day Israel. This makes a lot of sense to me because of how much God speaks about Mount Zion, referring to Jerusalem, and its association with the tree of life.

> It is like the dew of Hermon, descending upon the mountains of Zion; for there the LORD commanded the blessing—life forevermore.
>
> —PSALM 133:3

Where does God command life forevermore? The blessing of eternal life was commanded at Mount Zion, the only place of true unity because of the death, burial, and resurrection of Christ. So it is highly likely that the Garden of Eden and the tree of life were located in Jerusalem. Again, my research and the experts I have talked with, who are in the process of making their findings public, cause me to believe this is true.

If the Garden of Eden was in fact located in the area of Jerusalem, then that brings new light to a curious story in the Gospels. During Jesus' final days on the earth, immediately after His triumphal entry into Jerusalem, He had an odd encounter with a fig tree.

> Now in the morning, as He returned to the city, He was hungry. And seeing a fig tree by the road, He came to it and found nothing on it but leaves, and said to it, "Let no fruit grow on you ever again." Immediately the fig tree withered away.
> —MATTHEW 21:18–19

Nothing Jesus ever did was random, and everything had a much greater spiritual significance than a cursory reading of the text will unveil. Jesus wasn't simply creating an opportunity to teach on faith, which He does a few verses later.

I believe the spot Jesus was passing was also the place where He was going to be crucified. The experts I have spoken with have said that since we now know where the ancient temple really was and we know Jesus was lodging at Bethany, we also know the route Jesus took going back and forth. He crossed from Bethany over the Mount of Olives to Mount Zion. That would mean Jesus was crucified on the Mount of Olives at the exact spot where the red heifer was sacrificed to God to purify the Israelites of their sin (Num. 19:3; Heb. 13:11–12).

The experts I've spoken with also told me that with crucifixion it was common in Roman law that the offender be killed at the exact location of the offense. If the exact location of the crime was unknown, the person was crucified at the place where he was arrested. I want you to let that sink in.

Jesus was arrested in the Garden of Gethsemane, which was located at the foot of the Mount of Olives. So let's put this all together. If the Garden of Eden occupied the same area as Jerusalem, then something amazing took place. Jesus may have been crucified at the exact spot where the original offense had been committed.

That would mean everything that happened was prophetic—everything. From what these archeologists and experts have shown me, Jesus was likely killed on the exact spot where Adam and Eve ate of the tree of the knowledge of good and evil. Scripture says Jesus was crucified at Golgotha, meaning "Place of a Skull" (Matt. 27:33; Mark 15:22; John 19:17), and tradition has it located on the other side of the city. But translating Golgotha as "the Place of a Skull" is tricky. Scholars I've consulted say the term literally means the front part of the skull or head.

I believe there is a strong possibility that what it refers to is Adam as the head of all mankind. Jesus may have been crucified where the "head" of fallen man was located. This understanding, then, supports what I am saying here, that Jesus may have died at the same spot where Adam and Eve sinned. It's possible that the second Adam, Jesus, paid the price for our sins by dying upon the cross at the exact place where sin entered the world.

This is all incredible and worthy of much deeper study. But you may be wondering what this has to do with the fig tree. Consider the following passage.

> So when the woman saw that the tree was good for food, that it was pleasant to the eyes, and a tree desirable to make one wise, she took of its fruit and ate. She also gave to her husband with her, and he ate. Then the eyes of both of them were opened, and

they knew that they were naked; and they sewed fig
leaves together and made themselves coverings.

—Genesis 3:6–7

They sewed fig leaves together to cover their nakedness,
their shame. As we have previously learned, the fig leaf was
man's effort to cover and atone for his sin. It was always
destined to fail because our human effort cannot remove
the shame of sin; only the blood of Jesus can do that.

When Jesus arrived at the fig tree, Mark's Gospel says it
was not the time of the fig. Jesus was obviously intelligent
and clearly knew it wasn't fig season, but He went to the
tree anyway. The fig tree doesn't grow leaves until the fig
is ripe. The fact that the tree had leaves should have meant
it was bearing fruit, but it was barren. This is an incredible representation to us of the difference between man's
works and the finished work of Christ on the cross.

Jesus said,

I am the vine, you are the branches. He who abides
in Me, and I in him, bears much fruit; for without
Me you can do nothing. If anyone does not abide in
Me, he is cast out as a branch and is withered; and
they gather them and throw them into the fire, and
they are burned.

—John 15:5–6

Now read the following passage, bearing in mind that
Jesus said, "If anyone does not abide in Me, he is cast out
as a branch and is withered."

And seeing a fig tree by the road, He came to it and
found nothing on it but leaves, and said to it, "Let

no fruit grow on you ever again." Immediately the
fig tree withered away.

—Matthew 21:19

The word translated "withered" in both verses is the
exact same Greek word: *xērainō*.[3] By cursing the fig tree,
Jesus was pointing out the utter futility of our works and
efforts to atone for and cover our sin and shame.

Since Jesus was a direct descendant of Adam, it is also
my belief that this fig tree not only was located in the same
place where Adam and Eve sinned four thousand years
earlier but also was a direct descendant of the fig tree that
Adam made coverings with from its leaves. Man's works
can never remove his shame; thus, Jesus was showing us
that man's works—the fig leaves—were like a fruitless tree,
which He cursed forever.

Whether or not the fig tree was an actual descendant of
the fig tree in the garden, what is clear is that Jesus was not
engaged in some random act when He cursed the fig tree.
He was pointing us all to the fact that our efforts cannot
atone for or cover our sin or the shame of our sin.

WHY WAS SHAME THE FIRST MANIFESTATION OF SIN?

This is a vital point to understand. Shame will always
be the result when we get our eyes on ourselves. Eve was
deceived into engaging in the same foolishness that Lucifer
got involved with in heaven. Through its lies and deception, the serpent got Eve to get her eyes off God and onto
her own self-interest. All sin is rooted in self. Look again
at the account in Genesis.

> So when the woman saw that the tree was good for
> food, that it was pleasant to the eyes, and a tree desir-
> able to make one wise, she took of its fruit and ate.
> She also gave to her husband with her, and he ate.
> —GENESIS 3:6

The serpent did not tell her that God was lying to her. He told her, "You will not surely die. For God knows that in the day you eat of it your eyes will be opened, and you will be like God, knowing good and evil" (Gen. 3:4–5). Basically he was saying if you eat of this tree, you will receive a great personal benefit. You will be like God.

Eve listened, and as a result a series of events was about to unfold that would lead to a great shift. Adam and Eve were about to reject the very nature of God in a failed attempt to become more like Him. They were about to lose the image of God they were created with.

We read in Genesis 1:26–27:

> Then God said, "Let Us make man in Our image,
> according to Our likeness."...So God created man
> in His own image; in the image of God He created
> him; male and female He created them.

This leads to an important question: What then is the image and likeness of God? Many scholars and preachers throughout history have tried to define this. Some say it is man's free will; some say it's man's authority to have dominion; some say it's simply to show that man is distinct above all other creatures. These may all be true, but I think it's something much simpler.

> Beloved, let us love one another, for love is of God;
> and everyone who loves is born of God and knows

God. He who does not love does not know God, for
God is love....And we have known and believed the
love that God has for us. God is love, and he who
abides in love abides in God, and God in him.

—1 JOHN 4:7–8, 16

God is love. He isn't simply loving; He is the embodi-
ment of love. Jesus came to restore to us that very image
of God, and we see what that looks like in Paul's letter to
the Ephesians.

May Christ through your faith [actually] dwell (settle
down, abide, make His permanent home) in your
hearts! May you be rooted deep in love and founded
securely on love, that you may have the power and
be strong to apprehend and grasp with all the saints
[God's devoted people, the experience of that love]
what is the breadth and length and height and depth
[of it]; [That you may really come] to know [practi-
cally, through experience for yourselves] the love of
Christ, which far surpasses mere knowledge [without
experience]; that you may be filled [through all your
being] unto all the fullness of God [may have the
richest measure of the divine Presence, and become
a body wholly filled and flooded with God Himself]!

—EPHESIANS 3:17–19, AMPC

The revelation knowledge of the experience of God's
agape love is what causes us to be filled unto all the fullness of God and become a body wholly filled and flooded
with God Himself. Adam and Eve didn't simply eat of for-
bidden fruit. They violated the law of love.

THE LAW OF LOVE IS EXPRESSED IN THE WORDS OF JESUS

Jesus said, "Greater love has no one than this, than to lay down one's life for his friends" (John 15:13). Agape love is a decision of your will to act in the best interest of another person regardless of the consequences to yourself.

Agape love—God's love—always puts others' best interest above and before our own. Nineteenth-century revivalist Charles Finney described it as "disinterested benevolence." It is acting to benefit someone else above any regard to how it may benefit or harm oneself.

In a lecture on the attributes of love, Finney explained that "the very idea of disinterested benevolence (and there is no other true benevolence,) implies the abandonment of the spirit of self-seeking, or of selfishness. It is impossible to become benevolent without ceasing to be selfish."[4]

Finney said in other lectures:

> By disinterested benevolence I do not mean, that a person who is disinterested feels no interest in his object of pursuit, but that he seeks the happiness of others for its own sake, and not for the sake of its reaction on himself, in promoting his own happiness. He chooses to do good because he rejoices in the happiness of others, and desires their happiness for its own sake. God is purely and disinterestedly benevolent. He does not make his creatures happy for the sake of thereby promoting his own happiness, but because he loves their happiness and chooses it for its own sake. Not that He does not feel happy in promoting the happiness of his creatures, but that he does not do it for the sake of his own gratification.[5]

Finney preached on this topic many times, explaining in another lecture:

> Another peculiarity of this love, which must, by no means, be overlooked, is, that it must be disinterested, i.e. that we should not love him for selfish reasons. But that we should love him for what he is—with benevolence; because his well-being is an infinite good—with complacency; because his character is infinitely excellent—with the heart; because all virtue belongs to the heart. It is plain, that nothing short of disinterested love is virtue. The Savior recognizes and settles this truth, in Luke 6:32–34: "For if ye love them who love you, what thank have ye? for sinners also love those that love them. And if ye do good to them which do good to you, what thank have ye? for sinners also do even the same. And if ye lend to them of whom ye hope to receive, what thank have ye? for sinners also lend to sinners, to receive as much again." These words epitomize the whole doctrine of the Bible on this subject, and lay down the broad principle, that to love God, or any one else, for selfish reasons, is not virtue....
>
> By disinterested I do not mean that the mind must necessarily feel that it has no personal interest in the thing. But that the degree of self-interest that is felt should not be disproportioned to the interest which the mind takes in the matter, on account of its own intrinsic importance. In other words, if the mind's interest in it is selfish, the action or exercise, whatever it may be, is sinful. If it be not selfish, it is holy, although there may be a suitable regard to our own interest, at the moment of decision.[6]

When God created mankind in His own image, He created us in the image of love. We were a creation of His love, by His love, and for love. When Eve was deceived she put her own self-interest and her own desire to obtain knowledge and power above the desire to please God. Paul declares that "this 'knowledge' puffs up, but love builds up" (1 Cor. 8:1, ESV).

Adam and Eve violated the law of love, which is the greatest of all the commandments. Consider Jesus' exchange with some Pharisees.

> "Teacher, which is the great commandment in the law?" Jesus said to him, "'You shall love the Lord your God with all your heart, with all your soul, and with all your mind.' This is the first and great commandment. And the second is like it: 'You shall love your neighbor as yourself.' On these two commandments hang all the Law and the Prophets."
> —MATTHEW 22:36–40

We live in a day when false teaching has flooded the church. It claims that any attempt to please God is legalistic and religious. This false grace message fails to understand the very nature of agape love. Agape love desires the pleasure, benefit, and enjoyment of God above any self-interest. When you have agape love, you want to please and obey God, not so you can benefit from your obedience but so that God is glorified. Your desire is His pleasure, His benefit, His exaltation, and His glorification above all self-interest. This is love.

Once they violated the law of love and put their own interest first, Adam and Eve became self-focused, and shame came flooding in. They tried to cover their shame. They tried to punish themselves for their shame. They tried to hide from the voice of the One who created them, and they failed.

THE CONFRONTATION

> And they heard the sound of the LORD God walking in the garden in the cool of the day, and Adam and his wife hid themselves from the presence of the LORD God among the trees of the garden. Then the LORD God called to Adam and said to him, "Where are you?" So he said, "I heard Your voice in the garden, and I was afraid because I was naked; and I hid myself." And He said, "Who told you that you were naked? Have you eaten from the tree of which I commanded you that you should not eat?" Then the man said, "The woman whom You gave to be with me, she gave me of the tree, and I ate." And the LORD God said to the woman, "What is this you have done?" The woman said, "The serpent deceived me, and I ate."
>
> —GENESIS 3:8–13

The phrase "cool of the day" has been misunderstood. The word translated "cool" in this passage is the Hebrew word *rûah* or *ruach*, which means breath, wind, or spirit.[7] It is the word used to refer to the Holy Spirit in Genesis 1:2. You could say the Lord came to them in "the Spirit of the day," the day of the Lord.

God will always confront sin, for "there is no creature hidden from His sight, but all things are naked and open to the eyes of Him to whom we must give account" (Heb. 4:13). God came to expose what they had done, but instead Adam and Eve ran from God. Adam then explained why he hid himself, saying, "I was afraid because I was naked." In other words, he was afraid because he was ashamed.

Then God said the most amazing words: "Who told you that you were naked?" God was asking Adam, What new voice are you listening to now?

This is what the Lord spoke to the soldier in my vision:

> Adam heard Me as I came in the Spirit of the day. I came to him as I do to all whom I love. I came to expose the sin and bring them back to me. Having eaten of the fruit, Adam became filled with shame. He saw his nakedness. He was now more focused on his shame than on Me. He was now in a self-preservation mode. Run, hide, cover, accuse, blame—anything he could do to try to deal with the shame.
>
> The first words out of My mouth were to expose the shame. I said, "Who told you that you were naked?" I wanted to expose to Adam that the voice of shame was not his voice but the voice of another.

Adam and Eve violated the law of love, and shame was the result. They made a choice to benefit themselves above obeying God. Shame was the first enemy that came as a result of sin.

Shame can come from our own sins, but it also can come from being falsely accused. Shame comes through failures, false accusations, associations with others whom the world shames, and even from having been attacked and violated in our own lives. However shame tries to come, we too must answer the question, Who told you that you were naked? We must discern who told us to feel shame. As we discover these truths, we are going to begin down the path of breaking the curse of shame off our lives.

PART II

THE DEVIL
IS A LIAR

CHAPTER 4

THE DAY MY WORLD CHANGED

THIS WAS THE day I was dreading. As I stepped through the door into the downtown government building, feeling the warm sun on my back on this beautiful day, I knew I would not be experiencing this freedom again for six months. I was walking into the downtown jailhouse to turn myself in to start serving my six-month sentence. I was full of dread, fear, frustration, and a feeling of helplessness.

You see, I had just been convicted of a crime I had not committed. I knew I was innocent, and I knew given time I could prove it, but it was going to take too long and cost too much. I had resigned myself to the fact that I was just going to have to tuck my head down and try to get through these next six months.

After I entered the lobby of the building, I turned right and walked through cold, gray, metal double doors. I was heading to the guard station, where I would fill out some paperwork and be taken into custody and placed in the jail that was on the second floor. As I was filling out my paperwork at the guard station, which really looked more like an information booth, I noticed to my left a pile of those bright orange prison jumpsuits all the inmates wear.

I reached over and started to riffle through the pile to find my size. Just as I was picking one out, the guard said to me, "Oh, you don't need to wear one of those." I was shocked. What did he mean? All the prisoners wore those. I protested and told the guard, "Yes I do. I don't want to get into any more trouble. I just want to do my time and get past this horrible season of my life."

As I continued to pick up my prison garment, the guard said, "You don't need to wear one of those." Again I protested, even more adamantly. I told the guard I had been around prisons before, and I knew every prisoner must wear a jumpsuit. I emphasized that I didn't want any more trouble, and I grabbed the prison garment and stepped back over to the guard station.

The guard said to me, "I don't think you understand how dangerous it is up there. If you put on that garment, the guards will abuse you and the prisoners will mistreat you. But if you don't put that on, you can walk around up there free." I couldn't believe what this guard was telling me. It wasn't possible that he was right. I was going to be a prisoner, and I knew every prisoner had to wear that garment. I decided to ignore his words, so I took the orange jumpsuit, went into the public restroom, and changed into it.

As I was taking off my shirt, a father and his nine-year-old son walked into the restroom. The boy was very

54

friendly, had a huge smile on his face, and just seemed filled with joy and innocence. He quickly said a friendly hi to me, and I kindly said hi back. He then noticed the orange prison garment on the floor next to me, and his countenance changed. He became alarmed and fearful. He looked me in the eyes and with a trembling voice asked, "Are you a criminal?"

I emphatically said no. The boy pointed to the prison garment and asked me with trepidation in his voice, "Then why do you have one of those?" When he saw me without the prison jumpsuit, he was comfortable and joyful around me. But when he saw that bright orange prison jumpsuit, he was filled with fear. As I picked up the garment, I kept hearing the words of the guard, "You don't need to wear one of those. If you don't put it on, you can walk around up there free."

Then I looked in those innocent boy's eyes and saw his fear. I realized that I could choose whether or not to wear the prison garment, and whatever I chose would affect how I perceived myself and how others saw me. I decided in that moment not to wear the orange jumpsuit. I walked out of the restroom, and then *boom*, I was in my bed at my house, suddenly awake.

It was Sunday morning, January 28, 2018. At that time I was pastoring Zadok International Church in Keller, Texas. When I suddenly awoke from this dream, which felt very real, my heart was pounding. All the intense emotions of dread, fear, frustration, and helplessness were so real to me. I was so relieved it was only a dream, but it felt so real I couldn't shake the emotions.

I literally felt as if I had been through the trauma of being falsely convicted of a crime and almost ending up in jail. I started to pray and asked the Lord, "How am I going to preach this morning? My emotions are a wreck." I decided to draw a bath and try to calm myself down. The adrenaline was still coursing through my veins.

As I sat in the tub I pulled out my iPad and decided to review the notes for my sermon that morning. I had prepared a message titled "Breaking the Curse of Shame." As I reviewed my notes, still trying to calm down and shake off the nightmare, it suddenly hit me. What I thought was a nightmare was actually an incredible prophetic revelation—a revelation that would ultimately deliver me and many others from the curse of shame.

You see, this wasn't any ordinary Sunday. I was in the midst of the most tragic, life-changing event I had ever experienced. It was an event that had the potential to destroy my family, my ministry, my economic security, and even shake the faith of people around the world. It was an event that would bring me face to face with the destructive power of shame.

A LIFE-CHANGING MOMENT

A month earlier I was with two of my sons at the Onething young adult conference in Kansas City, Missouri. We had been there for three days. Fifteen times during the conference the Lord kept bringing a scripture before me. Sometimes I would feel Him prompt me in my spirit, other times I would see the verse in my mind's eye, and other times I would hear the still, small voice of the Lord saying it. Over and over, the Lord was drawing my attention to Psalm 138:8:

The Lord will perfect that which concerns me; Your mercy, O Lord, endures forever; do not forsake the works of Your hands.

The Lord has directed me to this verse many times through my more than thirty years of ministry. I know it well. However, I have learned that when God quickens a verse in your spirit, you should read it, pray it, and meditate on it. God is trying to speak something deep to you. Proverbs 25:2 says, "It is the glory of God to conceal a matter, but the glory of kings is to search out a matter." Many times God won't just reveal things to you. He wants you to search them out.

On December 30, 2017, just as worship was beginning in the 2 p.m. session at the Onething conference, I once again saw Psalm 138:8 in my mind's eye. I felt so strongly that I needed to read it again that I literally shouted out to God, "What are You trying to show me?"

I spent the entire hour-long worship time reading the verse, praying the verse, and declaring its promises over myself and, very particularly, my marriage and wife. I cross-referenced the verse, searched commentaries, and studied what I could. I was on a mission to understand why God had given me this verse fifteen times in three days. Less than five hours later, I would find out.

Around 7:30 that night, thirty minutes into the worship time, I checked my email and saw a message from my wife. She shared that she was having an emotional crisis and was at the brink of becoming bitter about everything and toward everyone, and she didn't want that to happen. She said she was taking a three- to six-month sabbatical from the church and ministry. She then dropped the bombshell: she had rented a house and moved out.

Ministry is much more difficult than people realize. I have watched people's demands emotionally crush many a pastor's wife. On top of that, we had adopted a troubled young man who struggled for several years with a horrible drug addiction. That season was incredibly difficult. I knew all of this was affecting her, but I wasn't expecting her to leave.

As I read the email I was overwhelmed with shock and sadness. How could this be? How could this be happening? I went to the bookstore side of the convention hall to try to compose myself. I went back into the service and grabbed my two sons, brought them into the back, and told them what happened. We were all stunned. We prayed. We didn't know what was going on or what to do.

I immediately started to call my spiritual coverings. When we started the church, I asked three outside pastors to be our spiritual oversight just in case some big crisis ever happened in the church, and boy was this a crisis. I asked for their prayers and sought their counsel. I wanted to know what to do, how to help my wife and our marriage, and what to do about the church. I volunteered to step down, take a leave of absence, and even resign the ministry. I just wanted to do what was right before God and what would help my wife.

I also added two other seasoned ministers to the counsel, and all five separately said the same things: Keep preaching; you don't need to resign or step down. Do not share with the church that she has moved out; only share that she is taking a leave of absence. And ask the church to pray for her.

I knew their counsel was correct, yet how could I keep pastoring? In my mind I was now a massive failure. What right did I have to preach the promises of God to the people? What integrity did my words have? I was losing my wife. I was losing my best friend and partner. I was disqualified!

More than what people would say about me, I was wrestling with what I was saying to and about myself. I wanted so much to protect her. I didn't want her to face public shame for her decision. My wife, who is incredibly introverted, didn't need to live out her emotional battle publicly. I tend to be an open book and extremely transparent from the pulpit. I am always sharing my struggles and failures. However, this time I knew that for her sake and any chance of saving our marriage, I had to remain silent.

I warned these pastors that the gossip in Dallas is vicious. People would find out we were living separately, and if they did, the rumor mill would explode, and that could cause great damage. They all understood but still insisted I not publicly share what happened. I submitted to my authorities and did as they said.

Unfortunately, my predictions were right. It wasn't long before the rumors began to fly. As a native Californian raised for eleven years outside of Philadelphia, I am used to people who say what they are thinking to your face. In the Deep South, the culture is different. They will often smile and talk sweet to your face, but behind your back they will shred you. I was in an impossible situation. How was I to protect my wife and yet be an open and transparent leader of the church? I had to choose to protect my wife even if I would be falsely accused.

Instead of people praying for healing and restoration

when they found out, some started to resent and withdraw. My character was now being attacked, and there was nothing I could do about it. I couldn't share everything because I had to protect my wife and give her room to heal. I couldn't privately explain the situation because nobody would ever come to me. I could see it in their eyes. I could feel it when we spoke at church: "Shame on you, Pastor Steve; shame on you."

People started leaving the church, all with the same claim: "God has told us our season is over." But I knew the truth. They didn't want to be around a pastor whose marriage was in trouble. They didn't want to be around a pastor they now thought was a liar. And the voices kept screaming in my head, "Shame on you, Pastor Steve; shame on you!"

AN ONSLAUGHT OF SHAME

After three months my wife started to attend services again. She seemed to be doing a bit better. She also became aware of the rumors and the damage it was causing the church. She told me she didn't want anybody to get hurt because of her actions. So after a few weeks she decided to make a statement to the church and try to explain what was going on. As I mentioned, my wife is an introvert, so for her to stand before the church and share her hurts and struggles was an incredibly difficult thing for her to do. I was amazed at her courage.

She stood up at the end of a service and read a multiple-page statement. She spoke about her emotional crisis and the pain she had endured in ministry and as a result of the family battles we had endured. She told them these things were pushing her to the brink. She then shared a few examples of things that happened in church life that hurt her deeply. She also shared that she never properly grieved after the sudden, tragic loss of her father just two years earlier. She was always the one to feel she had to be responsible to care for everybody, and she worked endlessly. In her statement she didn't share that she had moved out because that was too difficult for her. She cried the whole time she was reading the statement. It was difficult for her to be so transparent.

After my wife read the statement, some of the women of the church came around her and prayed. We both thought the worst was behind us and that she was doing better. I thought we might get through this season. However, no sooner had she read the statement than a new narrative arose: "How dare she blame us for their marriage problems!" Instead of being the merciful, restoring family of God, the church became a toxic environment. The poison of gossip and judgmental speech was polluting the church family. Satan was winning, and again the voices rose up, "Shame on you, Pastor Steve; shame on you. Shame on you and Pastor Carrie." I watched as this became a death blow to my wife.

Families left; leaders left; our name and reputation were being slaughtered, and there was nothing I could do about it. I was being convicted of a crime I had not committed. I was losing everything I had spent a lifetime building.

In July 2018, after a Sunday morning service, my wife handed me divorce papers. She had filed a contested divorce. In other words, there was nothing I could do to stop it. For her own reasons, she never wanted to try counseling. She was done.

Now that she had made the decision to file for divorce, I felt released to go before the church. I told them the entire story and then told them I was taking a two-month leave of absence. I was in no emotional shape to preach to them. Plus, to be honest, I didn't think I could face them the very next week. The voices were still screaming in my head: "Shame on you, Pastor Steve. Shame on you. You are a failure. Shame on you."

Some of the leaders closest to me began to say I needed to step down from ministry, possibly for good. I thought about taking at least a year off, but the spiritual authorities and counselors around me, which now totaled twelve seasoned, global ministers, were all telling me the same thing: "Keep preaching. You are innocent here. Don't stop the ministry." Even my wife said she couldn't live with herself if I left the ministry.

I knew that for the rest of my life some people would look upon me with judgment, and some ministry doors would close forever because I was now one of those "horrible" divorced people. And I knew other people would never again be able to receive the prophetic word that flows through my life. And so the chorus continued, "Shame on you, Pastor Steve; shame on you."

When people become disappointed and disenchanted with leaders, they will believe the most horrible things about them. Instead of following the Scriptures, which tell us to forgive, love, show mercy, always think the best, resist gossip, and so on, people will complain, slander, and destroy one another.

Over the next five weeks everything fell apart. The most horrible lies were spread about me. People who loved me turned on me, others wouldn't even speak to me anymore, and others still would call and yell at me. Some called me a liar and a coward, accusing me without ever telling me specifically what they thought I did wrong. Nobody ever asked me if even one of the rumors was true. Nobody ever told me what was being said. I went from being a beloved pastor and revivalist to an outcast.

By September 1, 2019, the once-thriving church I had led, a ministry known for revival and great moves of God, closed its doors. Then lies were spread about me on social media. False accusations and innuendos were leveled at me, and my reputation was being pummeled. Yet all along God kept speaking to me, "Keep silent and don't respond." Not everybody in the church turned against me. Some wonderful, precious saints just had to watch, wonder, and look to God for answers. After the church closed, only two people ever reached out to see how I was doing. Despite the multitudes we had touched with God's power, I was now all alone in my greatest hour of need.

Now my Book of Job type experience was complete. I had lost my wife, my church, my future, my friends, and my job. People were saying, as Job's "friends" did, "It's all your fault. Just admit it. All this happened because of you. Otherwise God wouldn't have let it happen." The voices kept saying, "Shame on you, Pastor Steve. Shame on you." However, something was happening inside me. In the midst of my valley of the shadow of death, I was learning how to break the curse of shame.

CHAPTER 5

THE CURSE OF SHAME

Back to January 28, 2018. After I woke up from the dream, I was in the bath just trying to get my mind off the dream and calm myself down. As I looked over the notes I had written for my sermon, "Breaking the Curse of Shame," the full interpretation of the dream flooded my mind. It was an instant download, and I immediately understood what the dream meant.

Even though God had given me this amazing prophetic dream, that didn't mean my battle was over. The dream turned out to be prophetic instructions for the valley of the shadow of death I had entered. The dream was warning me about the curse of shame.

Shame is by definition "a painful feeling of humiliation or distress caused by the consciousness of wrong or foolish behavior"; "a loss of respect or esteem; dishonor"; "a person, action, or situation that brings a loss of respect or honor."[1] In my dream I was innocent of the charges brought against me, but I was being judged as guilty. It is hard to express how real this dream felt to me. The emotions of dread, fear, and confusion as I surrendered to the injustice of this prison sentence were overwhelming. Yet each aspect of the dream revealed something vital for breaking the curse of shame.

THE SIX-MONTH SENTENCE

I had this dream just one month after my wife moved out. I had one month to realize the scope of what was happening and that if she didn't return every part of my life and family would be negatively affected. She said in the email that she was taking a sabbatical for three to six months, and I felt no matter what happened at the end of that season, I would be judged harshly.

In the dream I had just been sentenced to six months in jail for a crime I had not committed. I knew I could eventually defend myself, but the process would take so long and be so costly that I resigned myself to just suck it up, do my time, and try to move forward with my life afterward. I was going to bear the shame for something I hadn't done.

THE JAIL

As I entered the jail I walked over to the guard station to check in. The jail represented that time of life when I was going to be judged. The jail speaks broadly of those seasons we all go through when we are being judged. Whether we are truly guilty, falsely accused, associated with others who are guilty or falsely accused, judging ourselves for our perceived weaknesses, or feeling ashamed for what others have done to us, the jail of judgment is the same. No matter what the reason, the result is the same. You have been sent to the jail of judgment, and you are going to have to learn to walk free while in it.

THE GUARD AT THE CHECK-IN DESK

When I received the interpretation of the dream, I realized this guard was an angel. Angels aren't sent only to deliver us from things; they also minister to us as we go through things. We see this in the life of Jesus.

> And He was withdrawn from them about a stone's throw, and He knelt down and prayed, saying, "Father, if it is Your will, take this cup away from Me; nevertheless not My will, but Yours, be done." Then an angel appeared to Him from heaven, strengthening Him. And being in agony, He prayed more earnestly. Then His sweat became like great drops of blood falling down to the ground.
>
> —LUKE 22:41–44

The angel didn't deliver Jesus from the battle; he ministered to Him in the battle. In my dream the angel wasn't there to get me out of jail. He was there to make sure I was safe. He was sent to protect me from the curse of shame.

THE ORANGE PRISON JUMPSUIT

The orange prison jumpsuit was the key to understanding the entire dream. The prison jumpsuit was the garment of shame. It was what I believed I was required to wear because I had been judged guilty. I didn't see how there was any way out of wearing it. Though I was innocent, I believed I would have to bear the shame of one who had been judged guilty. I was convinced the guards in the jail upstairs would force me to wear the orange jumpsuit, and the other prisoners would make sure they put it on me. I didn't want to wear it but had to, or so I thought.

This part of the dream was so revelatory for me. I had come to accept in the month since my wife left that I was going to have to bear the shame of a failing marriage. People were going to judge me. I was going to judge myself. I thought, "I am a failure and will be judged unworthy of holding the office of a preacher of the gospel." I hoped that maybe, if given enough time, I would be able to recover somewhat from this jail of judgment, but it would take a long time.

When the guard warned me about the garment of shame, I just couldn't grasp how what he was saying could be possible. Everyone had to wear a prison garment, I thought. The jail of judgment demanded it. But the guard was trying to tell me there is a way to walk free even when the whole world has judged you. There is a way to walk free from the curse of shame.

THE PRISON GUARDS UPSTAIRS

While the guard at the check-in was an angel, the jail represented demon spirits. They were there to torment those who had on the garment of shame. As the angel at the desk tried to tell me, if I walked around up there without the garment of shame I could walk around free, but if I put it on the guards would torment me.

This truth is so powerful. When you put on the garment of shame the demons will pile torment after torment upon you. They will beat you with judgment and do their best to pile shame on top of shame. These tormenting spirits of shame only have power as long as you wear the garment of shame.

If you learn to break the curse of shame, these tormenting demons have no power over you. The battle with shame is fought in the emotions. Jesus has come to bring us into perfect peace. Just as the angels instructed in the prophetic vision of the end-time battle I shared in chapter 1, Isaiah 26:3 says, "You will keep him in perfect peace, whose mind is stayed on You, because he trusts in You."

These demons would have power to torment me only if I embraced the garment of shame. I had no idea how vital it was that I didn't put on the garment of shame.

THE OTHER PRISONERS

These were the ones who posed the most danger. They represented other people, often Christians, who were bound by the curse of shame. They wore their garments and were quick and eager to abuse anybody else they saw who was also wearing the garment of shame.

There is such a powerful truth here. The people who are most tormented by shame are often the ones to heap the most shame on others. It is one of the ways they try to cover their own shame. They attack others to deflect their own painful feelings of shame. This can be particularly painful and damaging when it happens within a church family.

THE BOY IN THE RESTROOM

This boy represented innocence and a person free of judgment. He looked upon me with no preconceived idea. He was friendly and open and ready to interact with me. He was blissfully unaware of my predicament—until he saw the garment of shame. The shame I was about to put on made him think I was deserving of that shame. When he saw the garment of shame he began to withdraw, stopped trusting me, and even became fearful.

When he asked me if I was a criminal, I emphatically said no, but he didn't believe me. Innocent people don't wear prison garments, he must have thought. When I saw his reaction and remembered what the guard kept telling me, I knew I had the power to choose. No matter what anybody else said about me, no matter what I thought was expected of me or what others would try to force on me, I and I alone had the power to put on or reject the orange prison jumpsuit. I chose the latter. I chose not to put on the garment of shame.

As the understanding of the dream flooded me, I saw that this was exactly what I was going through and would face for the foreseeable future. I was separated from my wife, and the situation might end in divorce. I was going to have to face church people, friends, critics, religious leaders, and the guy in the mirror. If you have been wounded in the house of your friends, I imagine you can relate. I love God's people, but as a whole churches in the West have produced gatherings not families. We haven't learned very well how to deal with the tragedies of life and balance the expectation that our leaders have a strong moral character with the reality that the devil loves nothing more than to tear a pastor's family apart.

Our cult of personality culture tends to place gifted and highly anointed servants of God on a pedestal of invulnerability. Some of this comes from the pulpit, but some comes from the pew. When our spiritual leaders face intense spiritual warfare, often the sheep are spooked.

Their image of invulnerability is shaken, and they respond in the flesh. They want to believe a person can walk close enough to God that they never suffer battles or defeats. And if someone does, something must be wrong with them. They must be harboring some secret sin. This is how people desperately try to make sense of it all.

How can a leader be so anointed, so used by God to lead so many other people to deliverance, and yet have a failing marriage? If he wasn't able to save his marriage, maybe everything he taught was false. These are the lies the enemy pummels people's minds with.

It is said that the church is the only army that shoots its own wounded. This is often true, but I want to submit to you that the biggest reason we shoot our own wounded is because we too are often tormented prisoners of shame.

Let me be clear here. I am not speaking about ignoring sin. All sin must be confessed and repented of. "Go and sin no more," Jesus said (John 8:11). Sin does have consequences. But thanks be to God for our Lord Jesus Christ, who shed His blood for the remission of our sins. If we confess our sins, He is faithful and just to forgive us of all our sins and cleanse us from all our unrighteousness (1 John 1:9). But Jesus didn't come just to forgive us our sins; He also came to deliver us from all our shame.

CHAPTER 6

HE FIXED ME ONCE, AND I BROKE AGAIN

I N SEASON 2, episode 6 of *The Chosen* series, Mary Magdalene made a statement after she had relapsed into alcoholism that has stuck with me: "He already fixed me once, and I broke again."[1] Both the scene and this line she spoke are all about the shame she felt when she returned to her old sins after Jesus had so miraculously delivered her. Even though this is not an actual account in Scripture, the writers of *The Chosen* have wonderfully exposed the real battles many believers face.

In the *Chosen* episode, Jesus sends His disciples Matthew and Simon to find Mary Magdalene after she disappears. When they stumble upon her, she is drunk, distraught, and filled with shame. They finally talk her into returning, but when she faces Jesus she proclaims, "I am so ashamed." Then she later says, "I just don't think I can do it."[2] Shame made her want to run and quit. It was robbing her of strength to endure. Shame was about to win in Mary's life and defeat the plan of God for her.

When I saw this episode I was deeply touched by how accurately the writers captured the battle with shame. When we fail, especially morally, the battle with shame can be very intense, and we will try anything to escape the pain of the shame.

In the Garden of Eden, Adam and Eve went through various processes to try to deal with the shame of their sin. They first grabbed the fig leaves to cover themselves, something we still do when we try to deal with shame in our own human strength. As we discussed previously, one of the manifestations of our human effort to deal with shame is modern hyper-grace teaching.

It goes like this: The grace of God has removed all law; as a result, Christians can't sin. No matter what you do, you are already forgiven; therefore, don't even be conscious of sin. They teach that the Holy Spirit never convicts a Christian of sin and that Christians, once born-again, never need to repent. I deal extensively with this dangerous and false doctrine in my book *Grace Is Not a Get Out of Hell Free Card*.

This teaching redefines biblical grace simply to keep people from feeling shame. Just as in the garden, it will never work. These teachings hinder saints from doing the only thing that can defeat shame, which is looking unto Jesus. The Word tells us to "strive to live in peace with everybody and pursue that consecration and holiness without which no one will [ever] see the Lord" (Heb. 12:14, AMPC). And it says, "Blessed are the pure in heart, for they shall see God" (Matt. 5:8).

Repentance is required when we sin. Our efforts to

remove the pain of shame by denying we have sinned or have any need for continual repentance is doomed to produce the opposite of freedom over time. Instead of truly producing a freedom from shame, it will only drive people further and further from the holy presence of God and His Word preached by His anointed servants.

> If we say that we have no sin, we deceive ourselves, and the truth is not in us. If we confess our sins, He is faithful and just to forgive us our sins and to cleanse us from all unrighteousness. If we say that we have not sinned, we make Him a liar, and His word is not in us.
>
> —1 JOHN 1:8–10

"If we say that we have no sin, we deceive ourselves, and the truth is not in us." Just meditate on that for a moment. There are those who try to claim that John was not talking to the saved in 1 John 1, but this is false. They claim this because their false grace message collapses under the weight of this truth.

I remember when I was teaching on true and false grace in my church. As I read quotes from one of the leading voices of this hyper-grace message, the congregation was in shock at what he was teaching. However, when I then told the church his name, everything changed. Seventy-five people left my church that day. They had been watching this preacher on TV, and his messages made them feel so good. They thought that believing this false grace message was going to once and for all relieve them of their shame and condemnation, but that just wasn't true.

The problem is this false grace message will not stand when the glory of God returns to the church. Just as in the

Garden of Eden when the Lord came to Adam and Eve in the "Spirit of the day," as we discussed in chapter 3, we too will discover that our fig leaves don't work, and we will be faced with the reality of our nakedness.

One of the most difficult parts of our Christian experience is knowing what to do when those who have been redeemed, delivered, and miraculously set free, and are living radically for God, fall back majorly into their old life. The shame of such a "fall from grace" can be so overwhelming it can keep them from ever returning to Christ. How we see shame, deal with it, and help others overcome it will be the difference between eternal life and eternal judgment for some. In my experience shame has kept more people who have fallen from returning to Christ and the church than any other single issue.

I have seen many such cases through my more than thirty-five years in ministry. I remember one extreme case in which a young man had been miraculously delivered from heroin addiction and two years later fell into crack cocaine addiction. I went into intensive prayer for him, and he returned repentant just five minutes after I prayed. The next day, after I spent hours more in prayer, the Lord told me to call him, even though I was overseas at the time.

The Lord told me to tell him that he was totally restored. As I spoke this to him over the phone, he responded with disbelief. He was truly repentant but filled with shame, fully expecting to be kicked out of the Christian home where he was living. He had always been rejected by his family, and now he had failed this Christian family who had accepted him into their home as a son. However, this family didn't kick him out but instead forgave and restored him.

I was personally involved in his restoration process, and

when I prophesied over him that he was fully restored, it took a while for him to accept it. When I got off the phone the Lord spoke to me, saying: "Do you want to know why I fully restore when someone returns to Me? This is how I defeat Satan. Satan will take sometimes years to tear a life away from Me, but I will restore in an instant. I never make people crawl their way back. The second reason I fully and instantly restore them is because if I don't, they are vulnerable to the enemy's attacks. I fully restore to defeat Satan and to protect My people from Satan."

Even though God may have truly delivered and redeemed a person, they can always fall away. We live in a fallen world with many temptations and demonic strategies. No matter how high we climb, no matter how powerful in the spirit we are, no matter how many gifts of the Spirit flow through us, we are always vulnerable to falling again. When we get our eyes off Jesus, even for a little bit, the dung of the world can begin to consume us.

In the episode of *The Chosen*, Mary had been miraculously delivered, but she still fell. When her past came to attack her, she felt fear and shame. The shame drove her away from Jesus and back to her old life. You may have experienced this yourself or have loved ones who have. Sin must be confessed and repented of; however, shame also must be fought. The shame of the failure can have a longer-term effect than the initial sin. Jesus came to forgive us from all our sins and deliver us from shame.

He fixed you once, but then you failed. Return to Jesus. Confess your sins. Be fully restored. Walk free from shame, for His blood removes all shame. Get your eyes on Jesus. He is closer than you think.

PETER'S DENIAL AND EXPOSURE

The story of the fall of Peter amplifies these truths so clearly. Peter had been walking with Jesus for three years. Can you imagine hearing the actual words of Jesus, witnessing His amazing miracles, learning how to pray from Jesus Himself, seeing Moses and Elijah on the Mount of Transfiguration, casting out devils and performing miracles yourself, and still denying Jesus? That is exactly what happened to Peter—the rock upon whom Christ would build His church (Matt. 16:18)—when he was questioned by a servant girl.

> Now Peter sat outside in the courtyard. And a servant girl came to him, saying, "You also were with Jesus of Galilee." But he denied it before them all, saying, "I do not know what you are saying." And when he had gone out to the gateway, another girl saw him and said to those who were there, "This fellow also was with Jesus of Nazareth." But again he denied with an oath, "I do not know the Man!" And a little later those who stood by came up and said to Peter, "Surely you also are one of them, for your speech betrays you." Then he began to curse and swear, saying, "I do not know the Man!" Immediately a rooster crowed. And Peter remembered the word of Jesus who had said to him, "Before the rooster crows, you will deny Me three times." So he went out and wept bitterly.
>
> —MATTHEW 26:69–75

Can you imagine failing so massively and publicly after having been so close to Jesus? Peter was so filled with shame that he fled from Jesus at His most desperate hour of need. Even after he had seen Jesus raised from the dead, Peter still fled to his past. He went back to fishing.

Then an amazing thing happened. This story is told in a passage of Scripture that has been misunderstood for years. Jesus came to Peter in his fallen state and brought the true process of restoration. Firmly grasping the restoration process revealed in John 21 is vital to understanding the nature and dealings of our God when we sin.

> After these things Jesus showed Himself again to the disciples at the Sea of Tiberias, and in this way He showed Himself: Simon Peter, Thomas called the Twin, Nathanael of Cana in Galilee, the sons of Zebedee, and two others of His disciples were together. Simon Peter said to them, "I am going fishing."
>
> —JOHN 21:1–3

Thomas, Nathanael, and the others went with Peter, and they fished all night but caught nothing. The next morning they saw Jesus standing on the shore, but they didn't recognize Him.

> Then Jesus said to them, "Children, have you any food?" They answered Him, "No." And He said to them, "Cast the net on the right side of the boat, and you will find some." So they cast, and now they were not able to draw it in because of the multitude of fish. Therefore that disciple whom Jesus loved said to Peter, "It is the Lord!"
>
> Now when Simon Peter heard that it was the Lord, he put on his outer garment...and plunged into the sea....Then, as soon as they had come to land, they saw a fire of coals there, and fish laid on it, and bread. Jesus said to them, "Bring some of the fish which you have just caught."
>
> ...Jesus said to them, "Come and eat breakfast."

Yet none of the disciples dared ask Him, "Who are You?"—knowing that it was the Lord. Jesus then came and took the bread and gave it to them, and likewise the fish.

—John 21:5–13

They ate breakfast, and afterward Jesus and Peter had a powerful exchange.

Jesus said to Simon Peter, "Simon, son of Jonah, do you love Me more than these?" He said to Him, "Yes, Lord; You know that I love You." He said to him, "Feed My lambs." He said to him again a second time, "Simon, son of Jonah, do you love Me?" He said to Him, "Yes, Lord; You know that I love You." He said to him, "Tend My sheep." He said to him the third time, "Simon, son of Jonah, do you love Me?"

Peter was grieved because He said to him the third time, "Do you love Me?" And he said to Him, "Lord, You know all things; You know that I love You." Jesus said to him, "Feed My sheep."

—John 21:15–19

Peter went back to his old life, leaning upon his old habits, though he already had been commissioned to minister. Jesus had commanded Peter and the other disciples to "go into all the world and preach the gospel to every creature," and He told them, "These signs will follow those who believe: in My name they will cast out demons; they will speak with new tongues; they will take up serpents; and if they drink anything deadly, it will by no means hurt them; they will lay hands on the sick, and they will recover" (Mark 16:15, 17–18).

Jesus had already rebuked the disciples for their unbelief.

He had already commissioned them to go into all the world. So why was Peter back fishing again? Often when we are dealing with shame we go back to what is familiar. We assume we are now disqualified from the destiny God has for us. We now feel inferior and insufficient for the task, and we retreat to the familiar.

Peter was not only returning to his past, but as too often happens he was influencing others. We have seen this time and again; when leaders fall away, often they take others with them. Shame tries to cover itself at times by gathering a crowd of others who also are hiding from the Lord.

Jesus, knowing that Peter was battling shame, went to him as the Father went to Adam. God never ignores sin. He always comes to expose the root of our sin and lead us back to truth.

Jesus said, "If you abide in My word, you are My disciples indeed. And you shall know the truth, and the truth shall make you free" (John 8:31–32). These verses reveal the condition to walking in the truth that makes you free: abiding in His Word. Only by abiding in His Word can you know the truth. So here we see Jesus, the Word of God made flesh (John 1:1), coming to Peter in the place he had retreated to.

Jesus didn't start yelling and condemning Peter. He did something truly marvelous. He performed a miracle that contained several key truths Jesus wanted to reveal to Peter and the other disciples.

Jesus first revealed Himself to Peter more than three years earlier and called him to be His disciple.

> So it was, as the multitude pressed about Him to hear the word of God, that He stood by the Lake of Gennesaret, and saw two boats standing by the lake;

but the fishermen had gone from them and were washing their nets. Then He got into one of the boats, which was Simon's, and asked him to put out a little from the land. And He sat down and taught the multitudes from the boat.

—Luke 5:1–3

Peter, then called Simon, had been fishing all night and caught nothing, and Jesus told him, "Launch out into the deep and let down your nets for a catch" (Luke 5:4). Peter did as Jesus instructed, "and when they had done this, they caught a great number of fish, and their net was breaking" (Luke 5:6).

Then in Matthew's Gospel we see Jesus calling Peter into ministry.

And Jesus, walking by the Sea of Galilee, saw two brothers, Simon called Peter, and Andrew his brother, casting a net into the sea; for they were fishermen. Then He said to them, "Follow Me, and I will make you fishers of men."

—Matthew 4:18–19

After Peter had betrayed Him, Jesus came to Peter the exact same way He first appeared. In doing this Jesus was sending three powerful messages. First, Jesus was telling Peter, "Even though you have denied Me and publicly failed Me, I have not changed My mind about you. I have not removed My call from your life. I still am going to make you a fisher of men, and I still am telling you to follow Me." What an amazing picture of our Master's love, kindness, grace, mercy, and longsuffering.

The second message Jesus was sending was that after His death and resurrection the supernatural would still happen, but He would not be physically with Peter. The first time Jesus performed the miracle He was right there in the boat with Peter. The second time Jesus was on the shore. In this He was signifying that though He was leaving, He would still be totally involved in His followers' lives. He was showing that even though He wouldn't be physically present as He had been, He still would provide.

The disciples, led by Peter, went back to their old lives after Jesus' death and were trying to provide for themselves instead of pursuing the Great Commission and trusting God for provision. Jesus will come to you in your darkest hour and still perform miracles of provision to show you that He alone is your source. He will show you that even in your shame-filled state He will never leave you nor forsake you.

A young man who had been miraculously delivered from years of drug addiction and was serving powerfully in ministry became hooked on heroine after a medical issue arose in his life. He publicly confessed what had happened before his church, but the shame of the failure was too great for him to continue attending services there. Instead of feeling as if he could be loved, accepted, and restored in the church, he ran. The church people were very kind to him, but they didn't understand how to help him overcome the shame.

For the next three and a half years he struggled with opioid and meth addiction. At one of his lowest points he found himself homeless on the streets of Anchorage, Alaska, in late September. Winter was arriving, and a cold, forty-degree rain was falling. Needing a place to stay warm and dry, he began walking in search of shelter. But he had only a light hoodie, so he was wet, freezing cold, and probably only hours away from deadly hypothermia.

Having not eaten for three days and fearing for his

life, he began to scream at God: "I thought You said You would never leave me nor forsake me! I am freezing and hungry, and I'm probably going to die tonight. You're a liar!" Screaming and cursing repeatedly at God, he said, "I hate You. I never want to see or hear about You ever again." He proceeded to use the foulest language to curse God. After his tirade he continued to walk, looking for some shelter. Then to his shock the Holy Spirit spoke to him and said, "Turn down this alley."

To his right was a long, dark alley. The Spirit told him, "Go to the trash bin at the end. There is a garbage bag by the right side. Open it." He was trembling with fear and awe. He thought, "I just cursed God, and now the Holy Spirit is talking to me?" When he got to the end of this long, dark alley, there was a trash bin with a black garbage bag sitting next to it. He opened the garbage bag and found a brand-new $400 waterproof ski jacket. The price tag was still on it. He quickly put on the jacket, only to discover under the jacket were boxes and boxes of gluten-free nutrition bars. This was such a precious miracle because he was allergic to gluten.

When this young man told me this story, I just cried. What an amazing Savior we serve. Even in our darkest hour, and in the midst of our deepest hurts, even when we lash out at God, He knows right where we are, and He is there for us.

This miracle on the streets of Anchorage reminds me of the miracle of the fish with Peter. Peter was in a bad way. He was filled with shame and leading others astray.

The third message Jesus sent Peter is the one we all must learn. This third message has been wrongly interpreted and caused much doctrinal confusion for centuries. However, if we don't understand this third message correctly, we will deal with our shame by going back to the fig tree instead of to Christ. The third message was shared around the fire.

CHRIST SPEAKS TO PETER

Let's look again at John 21.

> So when they had eaten breakfast, Jesus said to Simon Peter, "Simon, son of Jonah, do you love Me more than these?"
>
> He said to Him, "Yes, Lord; You know that I love You."
>
> He said to him, "Feed My lambs."
>
> He said to him again a second time, "Simon, son of Jonah, do you love Me?"
>
> He said to Him, "Yes, Lord; You know that I love You."
>
> He said to him, "Tend My sheep."
>
> He said to him the third time, "Simon, son of Jonah, do you love Me?" Peter was grieved because He said to him the third time, "Do you love Me?"
>
> And he said to Him, "Lord, You know all things; You know that I love You."
>
> Jesus said to him, "Feed My sheep."
>
> —JOHN 21:15–17

For years it has been preached that since Peter denied Jesus three times, Jesus came to restore Peter by getting him to confess his love for Christ three times. On the surface, when you read the account from an English translation, this is exactly what seems to have happened. But once you examine the story from the original Greek language it was written in, the entire dynamic changes.

There are two different words translated "love" in these verses. The first word is *agape*, which is God's supernatural love. The second word is *phileo*, which speaks of strong human affection and deep brotherly love. Man cannot produce agape love in himself; it comes from God.

Jesus said to Simon Peter, "Simon, son of Jonah, do you [*agape*] Me more than these?" Simon is a name that means "reed," an item that symbolizes weakness.[3] So Jesus said in essence, "Weakness, do you have God's supernatural *agape* love for Me?" Simon responded, "Yes, Lord; You know that I [*phileo*] You." He was saying he had deep, brotherly human love for Jesus. And Jesus said, "Feed My lambs."

A second time Jesus said to Simon Peter, "Simon, son of Jonah, do you [*agape*] Me more than these?" In other words, Jesus was saying, "Weakness, do you have God's supernatural *agape* love for Me?" Simon responded, "Yes, Lord; You know that I [*phileo*] You. I have deep, brotherly human love for You." Jesus said, "Tend My sheep."

The third time Jesus changed the question. "Simon, son of Jonah, do you [*phileo*] Me more than these?" Jesus wasn't asking Peter to confess his love three times; He was showing Peter the root of his sin. He was exposing to Peter that his human love, human strength, and human effort were never going to be enough.

Peter was the one who was so confident in his human strength and loyalty that he emphatically said he would never deny Jesus, even if everyone else did.

> Then Jesus said to them, "All of you will be made to stumble because of Me this night, for it is written: 'I will strike the Shepherd, and the sheep will be scattered.' But after I have been raised, I will go before

you to Galilee." Peter said to Him, "Even if all are made to stumble, yet I will not be." Jesus said to him, "Assuredly, I say to you that today, even this night, before the rooster crows twice, you will deny Me three times." But he spoke more vehemently, "If I have to die with You, I will not deny You!" And they all said likewise.

—MARK 14:27–31

Peter was very sincere in his belief that his intense human passion would be enough, but clearly it wasn't. When Jesus came to Peter at the sea and performed the miracle of the fish a second time, Jesus was saying to Peter, "I still have chosen you despite your sin."

He then did to Peter what our Lord wants to do with all of us. Jesus doesn't come to condemn or shame us, but He does come to expose the truth. For Peter to truly be free, he needed to know, agree with, and come into alignment with the truth, which is that apart from Jesus he could do nothing. Again, the only way we can ever truly be free is to know and align ourselves with truth. Jesus said in John 8:31–32, "If you abide in My word, you are My disciples indeed. And you shall know the truth, and the truth shall make you free." In other words, Jesus was saying, "If you abide in My word, if you keep your eyes focused on the revelation of Me, for I am the Word, then and only then can you truly be free."

Much of the modern teaching on grace leads God's children in an opposite direction from the key to truly walking in freedom. Shame will cause you to hide from the face of God. It will cause you, like Adam, to use man's methods—his fig leaves—to cover your shame. However, when you hear the voice of the One who has come to expose your sin, you will run and hide. Today we run and hide behind the bush called "freedom from a religious spirit." We have been told that the voice coming in the "Spirit of the day" is not the voice of God but the voice of a religious spirit. We have been told that the Holy Spirit would never expose or convict us of our sins. We have been told that those who, under the anointing of the Spirit, call Christians to repent are messengers of Satan. We then run and hide from the presence of God and from the preaching of the Word of God.

Peter, just like Adam, had to be confronted with truth. Peter, like Adam, now had an opportunity to receive the mercy and restoration of God. Peter, unlike Adam, responded correctly. Instead of blaming others for his sin, Peter humbled himself. He said, "Lord, You know all things. You know that all I have is *phileo*." Peter now understood that he was lacking the most important element to fulfill his destiny. Peter needed a baptism in God's *agape* love.

Peter needed the true baptism of the Holy Spirit. He needed to be baptized with the Spirit of truth. Only as we continue to look unto Jesus can we ever walk free from this demonic attack of shame.

CHAPTER 7

SHAME AND
THE CULTURAL
REVOLUTION

WE ARE IN the midst of a seismic societal shift that is being driven and empowered by the spirit of shame. This shift away from Judeo-Christian values into an atheistic, anti-Christ exaltation of man above and instead of God has reached a critical mass in recent years. Much of this began with the devastating *Roe v. Wade* Supreme Court decision in 1973, which legalized abortion.

In 1980 the Democratic Party took an official stand and gave its full-throated support for abortion in its party platform.[1] The Left and the media then began a shame campaign that continues today. The issue was reframed away from the rights of the unborn child into an issue of a woman's right over her body. If you were pro-life, you were accused of hating women, wanting them to be barefoot and pregnant, and relegated to the so-called pathetic role of a housewife. "Shame on you," the culture yelled. "You are anti-women's rights; you're misogynistic."

The media and the anti-God forces would then latch on to any attack against an abortion doctor or clinic and label all pro-life people as radical, dangerous terrorists. Their goal was simple. They wanted to make it shameful to be associated with the pro-life movement. Shame by association is one of the enemy's great strategies. If you support pro-life groups, then you are connected to abortion clinic bombers, the Left would say. So many Christians started to go quiet and resign themselves to living in a country where abortion on demand was the law of the land.

The strategy was then picked up by proponents of the radical homosexual agenda. They coined the term *homophobic*, which implied that if you speak or stand against homosexuality you are actually afraid of homosexuals. It was stated repeatedly that those who stand the strongest against homosexuality are secretly afraid of their own homosexual tendencies. So if you preach against homosexuality, it is because you are probably secretly gay. This shame attack put many into a defensive posture, and as a result they simply withdrew and started to keep quiet.

The media and the political Left would publicly harass certain high-profile Christians to intimidate the rest. They would also latch on to any Christian leader's moral failure as a sign that all Christians are hypocrites and have no true moral standing. In just a few short years we went from seeing homosexuality as immoral to considering it immoral to speak against homosexuality.

Scripture says, "Woe to those who call evil good, and good evil; who put darkness for light, and light for darkness;

who put bitter for sweet, and sweet for bitter!" (Isa. 5:20). Sadly, calling evil good and good evil has become a reality in our day, and it has succeeded because of the power of the weapon of shame.

Now that we have gone through a societal shift in the way we communicate, shame has a more powerful and dangerous platform. Social media has become the vehicle of choice to unleash the weapon of shame to beat Christians into submission and drive them into obscurity.

We fell into this trap, and now we are paying for it. We were told that social media was the new way to reach the lost and preach the gospel. We didn't realize we were submitting our message to platforms that would begin to censor and silence us.

We got excited at the prospect that we could voice our opinions unhindered while hiding behind our tech devices. We would no longer have to look people in the eye while we unleashed a torrent of random thoughts to the latest social media post.

We Christians, just like the world, became addicted to this new social form of interaction, often with an unfiltered approach to our communications that normally wasn't possible when we were face to face. People will post comments online that they would never say when in the same room with the person. So many used social media as a place to vent their frustrations because it felt safe. We could always ignore the replies to our rants and move on to the next conversation.

What we didn't realize was that the enemy was waiting in the shadows to unleash the weapon of shame in a way we had never seen before. The explosion of wokeness and the cancel culture is destroying our world. Now after years of unfiltered social media engagement, the purveyors of shame can use past comments to destroy someone in a day. CEOs have been fired, entertainers have had their shows canceled, politicians have had their careers destroyed, college students have been expelled, and many others have been beaten into submission to hyper-political correctness with ever-changing rules and standards.

Church leaders are terrified and have withdrawn from preaching on any hot-button topic for fear of being shamed. No longer do you need the power of the mainstream media or a political party to unleash this weapon of shame. Someone can repost an old tweet of yours, and within minutes it can go viral and the Twittersphere will come down on you like a swarm of locusts, with thousands of people joining in on the public lynching. People who are beloved one day can become the lepers of society the next day all because of the power of the weapon of shame.

Shame is being used to force people into accepting vaccines they don't trust, obeying COVID restrictions they don't agree with, placing masks on their children (who have almost no risk of death from COVID-19), and being separated from their loved ones under the guise of social distancing. Shame caused churches to remain closed, outreaches to be canceled, pastors to hide behind livestreaming services, and church members to be left alone and unprotected.

Grandparents were being told they couldn't see their grandkids unless they took the jab. Neighbors would chase you through a store yelling at you because you removed your mask. Politicians would blame all the economic problems on evil, unvaccinated conspiracy theorists. Shame, shame, shame, the crows kept screaming.

Shame on you if you don't support Black Lives Matter (BLM) or critical race theory; you must be a white supremacist. Shame on you if you want a secure Southern border; you must be xenophobic. Shame on you if you question election results and want election audits; you are a threat to democracy. Shame on you if you stand up to radical leftist school boards for teaching your third-grader about masturbation; you are a domestic terrorist. On and on it goes. The shame weapon is being unleashed to beat society into a new world order.

This is just the beginning. It's only going to get more intense.

"Blessed are you when men hate you, and when they exclude you, and revile you, and cast out your name as evil, for the Son of Man's sake" (Luke 6:22). To put it in modern language, "Blessed are you when society hates you because you stand for truth. Blessed are you when they cancel you. Blessed are you when they shame you and label you a racist, homophobic, xenophobic, ignorant, religious bigot." That's the Steve Foss version.

JESUS WARNED US OF THESE DAYS

Jesus warned us that difficult days would come. He told His disciples:

> Behold, I send you out as sheep in the midst of wolves. Therefore be wise as serpents and harmless as doves. But beware of men, for they will deliver you up to councils and scourge you in their synagogues. You will be brought before governors and kings for My sake, as a testimony to them and to the Gentiles. But when they deliver you up, do not

worry about how or what you should speak. For it will be given to you in that hour what you should speak; for it is not you who speak, but the Spirit of your Father who speaks in you.

Now brother will deliver up brother to death, and a father his child; and children will rise up against parents and cause them to be put to death. And you will be hated by all for My name's sake. But he who endures to the end will be saved.

A disciple is not above his teacher, nor a servant above his master. If they have called the master of the house Beelzebub, how much more will they call those of his household! Therefore do not fear them. For there is nothing covered that will not be revealed, and hidden that will not be known.

Whatever I tell you in the dark, speak in the light; and what you hear in the ear, preach on the house-tops. And do not fear those who kill the body but cannot kill the soul. But rather fear Him who is able to destroy both soul and body in hell....Therefore whoever confesses Me before men, him I will also confess before My Father who is in heaven. But whoever denies Me before men, him I will also deny before My Father who is in heaven.

—MATTHEW 10:16–22, 24–28, 33

The world will hate you when you speak the truth in love. They will speak all manner of evil against you and persecute you. This persecution is not relegated to physical attacks but is very often expressed through shaming you and your loved ones. In China they now track people's activities and give them a type of social credit score that determines what they can buy or borrow and the kind of jobs they can obtain. It's possible that if the government doesn't like what someone does, such as going to an underground church, they could lower that person's social credit score to punish him. If that doesn't change the behavior, they could begin to lower the social credit score of that person's relatives to punish him and shame him into government-sanctioned behavior.[2] This form of coercion and public shaming will spread throughout the world.

We see it already beginning to happen. Those who haven't received COVID vaccines are being publicly shamed. Government and popular figures are encouraging people to shame their unvaccinated family members into conformity. This is a form of brother delivering brother to death. Death is more than just physical loss of life. There is relational death, economic death, reputational death, emotional death, and more. The enemy will use societal shame to get people to reject Christ, the truths of the Word of God, and the work of God's kingdom.

It is already happening. Churches are flying the LGBTQ and BLM flags to appease the shame mongers. They're trying to prove they are not those intolerant, crazy, right-wing religious fanatics. They convince themselves that this is God's wisdom and we must grow with the times and adapt to the ever-changing culture.

Even in the church, if you preach holiness and radical surrender you are shamed as religious and legalistic. Societal and social shame have always been powerful weapons to impose ungodly restrictions on people and control them. Nazi Germany made the Jews wear a yellow star as a means of identification. "Shame on you; you are a Jew," the culture said.

This is the direction the world is heading, and the church will become a target. The onslaught of shame that is coming is unlike anything we have ever seen. We must learn to despise the shame, as Jesus did, or we will be defeated by it.

ARM YOURSELF WITH A
MINDSET OF SUFFERING

Therefore, since Christ suffered for us in the flesh, arm yourselves also with the same mind, for he who has suffered in the flesh has ceased from sin, that he no longer should live the rest of his time in the flesh for the lusts of men, but for the will of God.

—1 PETER 4:1–2

There is a suffering that comes when we truly stand for Christ. Part of that suffering comes when we are shamed. Shame is a painful feeling that comes from public humiliation. Shame can cause us to either shrink back in fear and retreat or overcompensate and react in anger and the works of the flesh. Only as we take on the mindset of Jesus can we walk in His freedom.

First Peter 4:2 gives us a glimpse into this mindset when it says "that he no longer should live the rest of his time in the flesh for the lusts of men, but for the will of God." The transition to despising the flesh begins with us no longer living for ourselves but for the will of God.

We are no longer living a life that only benefits us; we are living for what benefits God.

Jesus came to the place where the only thing that mattered to Him was to fulfill the will of His Father. He said, "For I have come down from heaven, not to do My own will, but the will of Him who sent Me" (John 6:38).

An internal shift must take place. Jesus was able to think so little of shame that it was unable to affect His behavior.

There is only one reason for this: He was not living for Himself. He was focused only on one thing, and that was to fulfill the will of the Father. Everything He did, said, taught, and performed was all under the influence and direction of the Father. When people rejected or shamed Jesus they were in reality rejecting the Father. Jesus even said in Luke 10:16, "And he who rejects Me rejects Him who sent Me."

> Then Jesus cried out and said, "He who believes in Me, believes not in Me but in Him who sent Me. And he who sees Me sees Him who sent Me. I have come as a light into the world, that whoever believes in Me should not abide in darkness. And if anyone hears My words and does not believe, I do not judge him; for I did not come to judge the world but to save the world. He who rejects Me, and does not receive My words, has that which judges him—the word that I have spoken will judge him in the last day. For I have not spoken on My own authority; but the Father who sent Me gave Me a command, what I should say and what I should speak. And I know that His command is everlasting life. Therefore, whatever I speak, just as the Father has told Me, so I speak."
>
> —JOHN 12:44–50

Jesus was able to not take the shame personally because He was focused on the Father and not on Himself. Let me state that again. Jesus was able to be unaffected by shame because His entire life, message, and works were all about fulfilling the will of the Father. He understood and was trying to teach us how to walk free from the voice of shame. He was looking unto His Father.

JESUS DECLARES THE SAME TRUTH OVER US

> He who receives you receives Me, and he who receives Me receives Him who sent Me.
> —MATTHEW 10:40

Your being received or rejected is not about you; it's all about Jesus. You may say, "But Brother Steve, Jesus was perfect, and I am weak and fail so often." This is why it is so important for us to learn how to walk free from both the shame of our real sins and failures as well as the shame imposed upon us by society. We are not our own; we have been bought with a price (1 Cor. 6:20).

The enemy will increasingly use shame to try to defeat us and cause us to walk away from our God-given destinies. The increase in public, societal shaming will continue until the end of the age. You will never avoid it by yielding to it. If you yield to the screaming crows of shame, you will fall back into bondage.

Many years ago I was in England preaching at a packed-out meeting. The Spirit of God was moving mightily. As I walked around the crowd praying for people, I came upon a woman in a wheelchair. Immediately the Lord told me to tell her to stand up, to which she replied, "I can't." I again asked her to stand up while extending my hand to help. She reached for my hand and stood up but still said, "I can't." As she now was standing in front of me, I told her to take a step. She again replied, "I can't," but took a step anyway. I asked her to take another step. She said again, "I can't," but took a second step. After we did this a third time, she suddenly shouted, "I can!" Then she took off running around the building completely healed by the power of God.

Her husband came to me at the end of the service and said, "My wife hasn't been able to get out of that wheelchair for five years, but I don't believe she's healed." I looked at him with dismay, as his wife was still running around the building. That night she came back to the service, still walking. She told me her husband kept demanding her to get back in the wheelchair or she would hurt herself. I told her to never sit back in that wheelchair again.

About six months later I preached at that church again. After the service started I saw the same woman entering in her wheelchair. I turned to the pastor and asked him what had happened. He told me a heartbreaking story. Every weekend her family would come visit, and all of them kept telling her to get back in that wheelchair lest she hurt herself worse. For six months her husband and kids kept shaming her, telling her she was endangering herself by walking in faith. For six months they mocked, ridiculed, and shamed her for believing that God had actually healed her, even though they all could see her walking. Just two weeks before I returned, she was so wearied by the constant shaming of her family she decided to sit back down in that wheelchair just to appease them. The pastor told me the moment she sat back down in the wheelchair she could never get back up again.

She lost her miracle because she yielded to the voices of shame. She was walking by faith every day, with her eyes focused on Jesus. But after simply trying to avoid any more shame from her family, she lost the divine flow of the miracle-working power of God.

Don't you dare sit back down in the wheelchair of your past, no matter how much the voices of shame scream at you. Don't sit down in the wheelchair of political correctness. Don't sit down in the wheelchair of wokeness. Don't you dare sit down in the wheelchair of public silence regarding your religious convictions. Only as we walk free from the voices of shame can we continue to walk in the supernatural life flow of God. Only as we continue to focus on Jesus, with our eyes fixed upon Him, can we walk in the power of the divine life of God.

The crows of shame will try to pluck out your spiritual eyes so you can't see Jesus. Shame robs us of our spiritual vision, and only as we see Him can we become like Him. It is time for us to begin the process of continually looking unto Jesus.

PART III

ALL EYES
ON JESUS

CHAPTER 8

LOOKING UNTO JESUS

I N THE VISION I shared in chapter 1, when the fallen soldiers rose up from the shallow graves filled with dung, they struggled to see Jesus. This caused more fear and panic, a sense of desperation, isolation, and even rejection. The angels told them to pick up their armor and present it back to the Lord to be purified. They also told them to ask for eye salve that they might see Jesus clearly.

The soldier who was being attacked by the crows screaming, "Shame!" was told to put on the helmet of the hope of salvation and to focus on Jesus and what He was focused on. As the soldier put on the helmet of the hope of salvation and focused on Jesus and what He was focused on, which is the end of the age, the noise of the battle and the screaming crows faded. Then and only then was he able to clearly hear the still, small voice of the Lord.

Again, we read in Hebrews 12:2–3:

> Looking unto Jesus, the author and finisher of
> our faith, who for the joy that was set before Him
> endured the cross, despising the shame, and has sat
> down at the right hand of the throne of God. For
> consider Him who endured such hostility from sin-
> ners against Himself, lest you become weary and
> discouraged in your souls.

The angels' instruction to the soldiers to ask for eye
salve directs us to the Laodicean church and the Book of
Revelation. John writes specific words of rebuke, encour-
agement, and correction to the seven churches in Asia
Minor. These seven churches were all located in proximity,
separated only by thirty to forty-five miles based on the
order of their mention in Revelation 2–3.

They were all under control of the Roman emperor
Domitian. Domitian was notorious for declaring himself
to be a god.[1] It is believed he was the first of the Roman
emperors to do so while he was alive, and he demanded
the people worship the emperors and the dynastic family.[2]

The Christians in this area were under intense persecution
and great societal pressure to conform to the new imperial
cult of emperor worship. Caesar Domitian was a foreshad-
owing of the Antichrist, who will rise in the end-time from a
restored Roman Empire. The Christians to whom John was
writing were facing the same kind of demonic assault, persecution, and exaltation of man the end-time saints will face.
John wrote the first three chapters of Revelation to prepare
the people for the warfare they were entering.

These same truths have been given to us to prepare
an end-time people to overcome during the most intense
period of wickedness and spiritual warfare the world will

ever see: the great tribulation. Now, you may say, "But Brother Steve, we won't be here for the tribulation, so what does it matter?" I have three responses to that.

First, what happens during the great tribulation will not just suddenly appear. Things are going to continue to get more and more intense as we approach that season. Second, even if we are not here at that time, our learning, studying, and walking in these truths will allow us to help prepare the generation that will face the coming global crisis. Third, a growing chorus of prophetic voices is aligning with historical Christian beliefs that the church will be alive and well during the great tribulation.

I know this causes a strong negative reaction from some, but just think about it this way: If you knew there was a possibility you were going to face three years of unemployment with no way of accessing welfare, how would you spend, save, and act differently today? Preparing yourself spiritually for the possibility you might be here during the coming global crisis can't harm you, and it might just save you. I would rather use all the tools and weapons Jesus has given us now so I can overcome, no matter what battles I may face.

If you train for a twenty-six-mile marathon and end up running only five miles, the race will be so easy compared with if you trained for only a five-mile race and had to run twenty-six miles. Prepare for the worst, pray for the best, and trust in Jesus.

With all this background let's look at the Book of Revelation and specifically the church at Laodicea. Most people are intimidated by the Book of Revelation and believe the main theme is the persecution of the saints. This is a far cry from the truth. Out of over four hundred verses in Revelation, only about a dozen deal with the persecution of the saints. The Book of Revelation's purpose is revealed in the first five words.

A REVELATION OF JESUS CHRIST

The overarching theme of the Book of Revelation is the revelation of who Jesus is and how He operates and that He is coming back to destroy everything that hinders love. Jesus is coming to rule and reign here on earth.

One of the great purposes of Revelation chapters 1–3 is to reveal thirty unique descriptions of the nature of Christ and eighteen eternal rewards for the overcomers and to remove the great hindrances to victory that have invaded the churches.

Although we are going to deal with only a few of these amazing descriptions of Jesus in these pages, I plan to address all of them in a subsequent book. The thirty descriptions I have compiled are:

1. Jesus (Rev. 1:5)

2. Christ (Rev. 1:5)

3. "Faithful and True Witness" (Rev. 3:14)

4. Firstborn from the dead (Rev. 1:5)

5. Ruler of the kings of the earth (Rev. 1:5)

6. He who loved us and washed us and made us kings and priests (Rev. 1:5–6)

7. He who is coming with clouds (Rev. 1:7; 3:11)

8. the One with a loud voice, as of a trumpet (Rev. 1:10)

9. the One with the voice as the sound of many waters (Rev. 1:15)

10. Alpha (Rev. 1:11; 22:13)

11. Omega (Rev. 1:11; 22:13)

12. First (Rev. 1:11, 17; 2:8; 22:13)

13. Last (Rev. 1:11, 17; 2:8; 22:13)

14. the One in the midst of the seven lamp-stands (Rev. 1:13; 2:1)

15. Son of Man (Rev. 1:13; Dan. 7:13–14)

16. the One clothed in a garment to the feet and girded about the chest with a golden band (Rev. 1:13)

17. the One whose head and hair are white like wool, as white as snow (Rev. 1:14)

18. the One with eyes like a flame of fire (Rev. 1:14; 2:18)

19. the One with feet like fine brass, as if refined in a furnace (Rev. 1:15; 2:18)

20. the One with seven stars in His right hand (Rev. 1:16, 20; 2:1; 3:1)

21. the One out of whose mouth went a sharp two-edged sword (Rev. 1:16; 2:12)

22. the One with a countenance like the sun shining in its strength (Rev. 1:16)

23. He who lives and was dead and is alive for-evermore (Rev. 1:18; 2:8)

24. He who has keys of the kingdom and the keys of Hades and of Death (Rev. 1:18; 3:7)

25. the Son of God (Rev. 2:18)

26. Holy (Rev. 3:7)[3]

27. True (Rev. 3:7)

28. the One who opens what no one shuts, and who shuts what no one opens (Rev. 3:7)

29. the Amen (Rev. 3:14)

30. the Beginning of the creation of God (Rev. 3:14)

The greatest weapon against shame you will ever have is to see Jesus as He is. Until you see Jesus as He is, you will never see yourself correctly. This failure to see Jesus is why shame is still so dominant in God's people and what makes us exceptionally vulnerable to the manipulations of Satan.

Much of our biblically based teaching in the Western church today is centered on who we are in Christ, what benefits we have received from God, and how what Jesus has done will empower us to have a happy and prosperous life here on earth. I say biblically based teaching because there is also a flood tide of self-help, psychological, humanistic, and culturally based teaching coming from the pulpits that has very little to do with the gospel.

However, even in the churches that do teach good doctrine and focus on the Scriptures, most of the sermons are about how the Bible helps us have a happy, more content, successful life. They teach us how to have a healthy marriage, how to overcome adversity, how to succeed financially, how to deal with disappointment, and on and on the series go. We are told that a good sermon must show people how Scripture can help them have a better life now.

These sermons do have a place in our Christian experience, but they will never give you the power you need to face the most intense season the world will ever face. Just look at what has happened to churches with the relatively mild COVID-19 pandemic. I describe it as relatively mild because other global pandemics caused far more deaths, such as the Black Death, which is believed to have wiped out a third of the population of Europe in the mid-fourteenth century and roughly twenty-five million people worldwide.[4] Compare this with the total deaths from COVID-19. As of December 15, 2021, the global death toll reported to the World Health Organization was 5,324,969[5] out of a population of 7,875,000,000.[6] That's less than 0.07 percent.

COVID-19 hit, and the church shuttered. Many churches, months after opening back up, still struggle to get more than 50 percent of their congregation to participate in person. Fear, panic, selfishness, infighting, backbiting, slander, betrayal, and so much more became prevalent during the pandemic. If our teaching is so powerful and effective, then why did the church crumble under a global crisis that was nothing in comparison with what is about to come upon the world? I will submit to you that the huge focus on who we are instead of who Jesus is has led to this apparent weakness in God's people. We were so easily overcome with fear and yielded to carnal rationale to justify our fear that it exposed our desperate need for a much deeper revelation of Christ.

BEHOLDING HIM IN THE WORD

> And all of us, as with unveiled face, [because we] continued to behold [in the Word of God] as in a mirror the glory of the Lord, are constantly being transfigured into His very own image in ever increasing splendor and from one degree of glory to another; [for this comes] from the Lord [Who is] the Spirit.
>
> —2 Corinthians 3:18, ampc

In churches across the nation much focus has been put on getting people to see who they are in Christ. Second Corinthians 3:18 tells us how spiritual transformation happens. We are not changed as we look into the Word of God to see who we are. We are changed as we look into the Word of God to behold the glory of the Lord.

This is no small point. Teaching people about the benefits of following Jesus is not what transforms them from glory to glory. It is as we see Jesus in His glory that we are truly transformed into His image. The focus is to be on Him, not on us.

We need to look toward and unto Jesus, the Word of God made flesh, to behold Him as He is. This is more than just teachings, more than just memorizing scriptures. This requires a supernatural empowerment by God to give us eyes to see.

THE CHURCH AT LAODICEA

> And to the angel of the church of the Laodiceans write, "These things says the Amen, the Faithful and True Witness, the Beginning of the creation of God: I know your works, that you are neither cold

nor hot. I could wish you were cold or hot. So then, because you are lukewarm, and neither cold nor hot, I will vomit you out of My mouth. Because you say, 'I am rich, have become wealthy, and have need of nothing'—and do not know that you are wretched, miserable, poor, blind, and naked—I counsel you to buy from Me gold refined in the fire, that you may be rich; and white garments, that you may be clothed, that the shame of your nakedness may not be revealed; and anoint your eyes with eye salve, that you may see. As many as I love, I rebuke and chasten. Therefore be zealous and repent.

"Behold, I stand at the door and knock. If anyone hears My voice and opens the door, I will come in to him and dine with him, and he with Me. To him who overcomes I will grant to sit with Me on My throne, as I also overcame and sat down with My Father on His throne. He who has an ear, let him hear what the Spirit says to the churches."

—REVELATION 3:14–22

What a powerful and stern rebuke from our Lord. Jesus starts off by declaring three descriptions of Himself: "the Amen, the Faithful and True Witness, [and] the Beginning of the creation of God." By declaring that He is the "Amen," He is saying He's the final word, the certainty, and the truth. He is the "So Let It Be Done," which means once He speaks, it's over. Whatever He says is guaranteed; it's a certainty.

He also proclaims Himself the "Faithful and True Witness." Everything He says and does is in perfect alignment with the will and words of the Father. You need to understand His words are the final words.

Then He declares Himself to be the "Beginning of the creation." What an incredible statement. He wasn't just there at the beginning; He *is* the beginning.

> In the beginning was the Word, and the Word was with God, and the Word was God. He was in the beginning with God. All things were made through Him, and without Him nothing was made that was made. In Him was life, and the life was the light of men.
>
> —JOHN 1:1–4

Jesus was declaring to Laodicea that what He was about to say was absolute—final—and He had the authority to back it up. He had every right to declare it since everything was created through Him.

Then He goes on to rebuke them for their compromise. He calls it lukewarmness. He is speaking here of mixture. Laodicea had no natural water source, so it used a series of aqueducts to transport water in. One such aqueduct came from the nearby town of Hierapolis. The hot mineral springs that came from this region were widely believed to have healing and restorative power. The springs were loaded with lime and not very good for drinking but were great for soaking and bathing. There also were fresh cold-water springs in the nearby town of Colossae. This would provide drinking water.[7]

When Jesus said He would rather we be hot or cold, He wasn't saying He would rather we be on fire for God or completely hardened. He was pointing out that both Hierapolis and Colossae had water that was useful, but if you mixed the two and tried to drink it, the water wasn't any good. In essence Jesus was saying mixture and compromise were making the church useless.

Laodicea was a hub of commerce, trade, and banking. As such it was wealthy and powerful. Caesar Domitian had declared himself to be a god and demanded to be worshipped. Refusal to worship Caesar was met with strong persecution and an inability to buy and sell. Rome threatened the Christians with economic punishment if they did not worship the emperor.

It is clear from Jesus' rebuke that the Christians at Laodicea had convinced themselves they could worship Jesus and still be acceptable to Rome. They had engaged in mixture. We don't know for sure how this looked, but it is clear they believed they were still serving God faithfully despite their compromise, and they pointed to their prosperity to prove it to themselves.

Jesus ripped this lie apart in one sentence, telling the Laodicean church, "Because you say, 'I am rich, have become wealthy, and have need of nothing'—and do not know that you are wretched, miserable, poor, blind, and naked..." (Rev. 3:17).

They didn't know their true, desperate spiritual condition because of their apparent wealth, fame, and prosperity. They believed they had all they needed materially and spiritually. This same arrogance and overconfidence can be seen in much of the Western church today.

We have huge buildings, big ministries, and massive media platforms and live in countries with more wealth than ancient kings could even imagine. We have plenty of food, fresh water, cars, phones, the internet, social safety nets, health care, and medicines unlike anything in history. On top of this we spend our short, hour-long church services giving little pep talks, telling people everything is all right. We tell them not to worry about their sin; God understands. It's all under the blood; Jesus only wants His people to be happy.

We avoid preaching about abortion, the LGBTQ agenda, political corruption, adultery, sexual perversion, greed, foul language, worldly entertainment, and the like. The gods of this world have declared, like Caesar of old, "Worship me and my system, or you can't prosper."

So instead of addressing the massive idolatry in our congregations, we entice people with pleasing, self-focused sermons to keep them coming to our services. Career, success, entertainment, family, friends, and the world's acceptance have become far more important than the pure, holy, consecrated, self-sacrificing life Jesus has truly called us to.

We think because we go to a church service, sing a few songs, listen to a self-help message, and call ourselves Christians, we haven't compromised. "Who, me? I'm not engaged in idolatry," we say. "I'm blessed and highly favored of the Lord." Yet when a small trial called COVID-19 hit, we ran for the hills. We cowered under the pressure of society, took on their rhetoric, confessed their fear, attacked fellow believers for their refusal to "accept the science," and ultimately denied the Lord by denying His power.

The great goal of Christianity is not to avoid dying. We are commanded—not requested but commanded—to not forsake the gathering of ourselves together.

> Let us hold fast the confession of our hope without wavering, for He who promised is faithful. And let us consider one another in order to stir up love

and good works, not forsaking the assembling of
ourselves together, as is the manner of some, but
exhorting one another, and so much the more as
you see the Day approaching.

—HEBREWS 10:23–25

Much of the Western church did not hold fast the confession of their hope; they did not consider one another as
more important than themselves; they did not continue
to gather together but believed the lie that streaming their
services online was good enough. We are clearly commanded to gather together and all the more so as we see
the day approaching. No matter what the government or
society says or how difficult the circumstances are, the
church needs to be together.

I was so blessed in 2020–21 as I met the remnant. Through
a series of divine encounters I met pastors, leaders, and
church members who understood that being faithful to the
Word was more important than our individual safety or
financial security. I met pastors such as Ché Ahn of Harvest
Rock Church in Pasadena, California, who was repeatedly
threatened with jail time if he continued to have in-person
church services. He stood fast, held his ground, fought
legal battles all the way to the Supreme Court, and won.
He kept the doors of his church open, defying local government leaders, because he understood Christians need to
gather together. Because of his courage, the Supreme Court
of the United States reaffirmed churches' right to stay open
even during a pandemic.

Evangelist Mario Murillo conducted open-air tent
revivals while being ordered not to. He was willing to risk
his ministry, freedom, and finances to bring the gospel

to the drug addict, homeless, and brokenhearted. I met many others nobody will ever know who stood fast like the church of Smyrna.

> And to the angel of the church in Smyrna write, "These things says the First and the Last, who was dead, and came to life: 'I know your works, tribulation, and poverty (but you are rich); and I know the blasphemy of those who say they are Jews and are not, but are a synagogue of Satan. Do not fear any of those things which you are about to suffer. Indeed, the devil is about to throw some of you into prison, that you may be tested, and you will have tribulation ten days. Be faithful until death, and I will give you the crown of life.'"
> —REVELATION 2:8–10

Every one of the pastors I met said the same thing. They told me stories of being attacked on social media and in person by Christians and other pastors who would shame them. These brave ministers were accused of being rebellious, cavalier about people's lives and safety, selfish, in it only for the money, and many other things. The voice of shame was screaming at them to get them to compromise, but they wouldn't. Some lost members; some were arrested; some have been removed from social media platforms; some have lost friends and family. But like Smyrna they wouldn't compromise.

Laodicea, on the other hand, did compromise. They operated in a way that caused Rome to leave them alone. They convinced themselves that their prosperity, church size, and positive reputation in the community were signs of God's favor when they weren't.

I remember being awakened by the Spirit of God many years ago. He said, "Many of My people and My preachers misunderstand My favor. They think crowds, money, access to powerful people, and fame are signs of My favor upon their lives personally." God said, "I will give favor to a ministry to fulfill My plans and purposes, but that is not how you are to ever judge My favor upon your life. My favor on your life is only ever to be measured by one thing: the access I have given you to My presence."

The lukewarm church is not a quiet church or a dead church. It can appear to have fire and life. But it is a compromising church. When you hear dynamic, prophetic, expressive services on Sunday but go out and watch every form of R-rated movie, use foul language, get drunk, party at the clubs, and engage in the works of the flesh, you are Laodicea.

If you are sleeping with your girlfriend or boyfriend, have embraced the woke cancel culture, and refuse to call sin *sin* but attend a famous Holy Ghost church or conference and think you are in God's army, you are Laodicea.

If at one moment you are singing the latest hit worship song and then driving home singing along to the vilest rap song, you are Laodicea. If you choose not to call out sin from the pulpit or address the horrors of abortion and call all holiness preachers religious, you are Laodicea.

The church at Laodicea seemed to have God's favor but did not have a revelation of who God is, nor did they have access to Him. Feeling the presence of God is a far cry from truly having access to His presence. Access to His presence entails beholding Him in His glory. It is seeing Jesus as He really is. It will always produce an internal change and an external change of behavior. If your outward behavior hasn't changed, then you haven't really had a revelation of God.

Unfortunately some will say, "Brother Steve, you are not being loving like Christ. The Holy Spirit doesn't convict Christians of sin because we are already forgiven." The Laodiceans may have believed the same thing, but Jesus set the record straight when He told them, "As many as I love, I rebuke and chasten. Therefore be zealous and repent" (Rev. 3:19).

Jesus is revealing to the compromising church that they are not experiencing His real presence, the kind of manifestation that causes us to be changed from glory to glory. Jesus said to the Laodiceans, "Behold, I stand at the door and knock. If anyone hears My voice and opens the door, I will come in to him and dine with him, and he with Me" (Rev. 3:20).

Shame always was and is a massive weapon in the hands of the enemy to manipulate God's people into disobedience. Today we see the societal pressure of shame on Christian business owners who refuse to celebrate the LGBTQ lifestyle or those who won't take on the banner and rhetoric of BLM. We see many churches embracing the lies of critical race theory and the social gospel. This massive Laodicean compromise has come today because we have heard the decree of "Caesar." The gods of this world—Big Tech, media, and government—have threatened our businesses, churches, social media pages, and good reputations if we don't accept their new gospel of social justice.

Yet because Jesus loves us and His church, He is coming with a strong rebuke as well as a clear answer and invitation. Jesus is standing at the door right now and knocking. Will you repent and let Him in? Will you be willing to discard your culturally compromised view of Jesus and risk seeing Him as He really is? Only the true revelation of Jesus Christ—a focus on Him and what He is focused on—will give you the strength you'll need to overcome in the last days.

CHAPTER 9

EYE SALVE

A s I mentioned previously, in the vision recounted in chapter 1 the angel instructed the fallen soldiers to ask for eye salve. This was a direct reference to Revelation 3:18:

> I counsel you to buy from Me gold refined in the fire, that you may be rich; and white garments, that you may be clothed, that the shame of your nakedness may not be revealed; and anoint your eyes with eye salve, that you may see.

The eye salve mentioned in this verse is a reference to a famous medicine in Laodicea that was supposed to bring health to the eyes. Jesus was using this illustration to speak of the Laodiceans' need of something to remove their spiritual blinders.

The reference to eye salve in Revelation 3:18 points us to the need for something supernatural from God to clearly see.

> But as it is written: "Eye has not seen, nor ear heard, nor have entered into the heart of man the things which God has prepared for those who love Him." But God has revealed them to us through His Spirit. For the Spirit searches all things, yes, the deep things of God.
>
> —1 CORINTHIANS 2:9–10

Paul consistently pointed God's people to the need for a supernatural anointing to see clearly.

> [For I always pray to] the God of our Lord Jesus Christ, the Father of glory, that He may grant you a spirit of wisdom and revelation [of insight into mysteries and secrets] in the [deep and intimate] knowledge of Him, by having the eyes of your heart flooded with light, so that you can know and understand the hope to which He has called you, and how rich is His glorious inheritance in the saints (His set-apart ones).
>
> —EPHESIANS 1:17–18, AMPC

Paul was praying by the direction of the Holy Spirit that you and I would receive a supernatural anointing of insight into the mysteries and secrets of God. Paul was praying for the most spiritual people of his day, a people who would later be rebuked in Revelation 2:1–5 for having lost their first love. The Book of Ephesians was written more than thirty years before Revelation, yet Paul points them to the same truth, which is a need for a greater anointing from God to see Jesus as He really is.

Ephesians 1:18 is often misunderstood. The New King James Version says it this way: "The eyes of your understanding being enlightened; that you may know what is the hope of His calling." Notice the verse says "the hope of

His calling"—not the hope of your calling here on earth but the hope of His calling. We will never rightly understand who we are and our role in God's great master plan until we understand who Jesus is and His calling.

> Beloved, now we are children of God; and it has not yet been revealed what we shall be, but we know that when He is revealed, we shall be like Him, for we shall see Him as He is. And everyone who has this hope in Him purifies himself, just as He is pure.
> —1 JOHN 3:2–3

This is such an incredible truth. When we see Him as He is, we shall become like Him. "And all of us, as with unveiled face, [because we] continued to behold [in the Word of God] as in a mirror the glory of the Lord, are constantly being transfigured into His very own image" (2 Cor. 3:18, AMPC).

We have a desperate need for the spirit of wisdom and revelation Paul speaks of in Ephesians 1:17. We must come humbly before God, recognizing that having head knowledge isn't enough. We need a supernatural impartation of spiritual eyesight.

The first time this exploded in my life was early 1987. I was listening to a message by Dr. Morris Cerullo on unity in the Spirit. In the message, he preached for about six minutes on Ephesians 1:17–18. I was so stirred by his words that I rewound the cassette tape and listened to it again. Once again something was stirring in me, so I rewound it over and over again, listening to the teaching, praying in tongues, and asking God to give me understanding.

I did this for two hours. When my roommate came home, I tried to explain to him what I was perceiving, but I became overwhelmed and just covered my face with my

Bible. It took me five minutes to regain my composure. I tried again to explain the revelation I was receiving, but once more I was overwhelmed and covered my face with my Bible. I couldn't seem to speak. I tried a third time to explain, and this time as I became overwhelmed, I suddenly was taken into an open vision.

I was standing in a vast expanse and saw these words floating in the air: "That the God of our Lord Jesus Christ, the Father of glory, may give to you the spirit of wisdom and revelation in the knowledge of Him." From within the words—not from behind or in front but from within the very words themselves—I saw the most amazing blue-white light. I knew it was the visible glory of God. I fell to my knees, crying out, "I see it; I see it." Then I heard the voice of the Lord loudly say to me, "Son, through My Word you will see Me."

That day a supernatural gift of God was imparted into my life. It was an anointing from God to see Jesus as He is in the deep and intimate knowledge of God. This same gift of God is available to all God's children. We have not because we ask not, and when we ask, we ask for selfish purposes.

I want you to long for the revelation of the deep and intimate knowledge of God, not so you can brag, boast, or have some special insight to wow people with. I want you to desire to see Him as He is so you can become like Him.

Paul expressed it this way: "That I may know Him and the power of His resurrection, and the fellowship of His sufferings, being conformed to His death" (Phil. 3:10). This longing to know Jesus can be so strong that even if it requires you to suffer greatly, including dying, you are willing because of the "excellence of the knowledge of Christ Jesus [our] Lord" (Phil. 3:8).

The eye salve speaks of this spirit of wisdom and revelation that gives us supernatural vision to see God as He is so we can be transformed into His image. I will say this again and again: the focus is not on who we are but on who He is. Only as we see Him as He is can we properly see and understand who He is causing us to become.

You can't make an accurate copy of a painting based on partial or blurred images. You must see the original closely so you can painstakingly make an exact duplicate. If you are in ministry, I pray you especially take this to heart. We ministers are called to build the body of Christ in accordance with the pattern of the original. How can we do this if we ourselves are so blinded by ambition, greed, selfishness, worldliness, cultural appropriations, and fear of shame?

God commanded Moses and the artisans who built the temple, "See that you make all things according to the pattern shown you on the mountain" (Heb. 8:5; see also Exodus 25:40). Moses was commanded to build the tabernacle according to the divine revelation he received on the mountain. We can build up other people's lives properly only as we have received revelation on the mountain of God's glory. Unless we climb high into the secret place of the Most High, we will never truly become like Him and be able to help others be transformed also.

SPIRITUAL BLINDNESS

What causes a Christian who once strongly pursued God, His holiness, and righteous living to become spiritually blind? There are many reasons given in Scripture, from pride to compromise to unforgiveness, but one major cause is the failure to focus on the second coming of Christ.

Beloved, I now write to you this second epistle (in both of which I stir up your pure minds by way of reminder), that you may be mindful of the words which were spoken before by the holy prophets, and of the commandment of us, the apostles of the Lord and Savior, knowing this first: that scoffers will come in the last days, walking according to their own lusts, and saying, "Where is the promise of His coming? For since the fathers fell asleep, all things continue as they were from the beginning of creation." For this they willfully forget: that by the word of God the heavens were of old, and the earth standing out of water and in the water, by which the world that then existed perished, being flooded with water. But the heavens and the earth which are now preserved by the same word, are reserved for fire until the day of judgment and perdition of ungodly men.

—2 Peter 3:1–7

Paul says in the last days a scoffing spirit will come. To scoff is to belittle, scorn, mock, harass, ridicule, or tease. Scoffing is a form of shaming. This passage is warning that in the last days scoffing and shaming will intensify because people will no longer believe Jesus is coming back.

Although much of this will flow from the world, this is already prevalent in the church. We might not publicly say, "Where is the promise of His coming?" but our actions show that we have no real expectation of the soon return of Jesus. Some even dismiss the truth that God will judge the wicked and cast them into a lake of fire.

This spiritual blindness comes from a failure to keep our eyes focused on what Jesus is focused on. Scripture warns strongly about the danger of spiritual blindness and slumber.

But if that evil servant says in his heart, "My master is delaying his coming," and begins to beat his fellow servants, and to eat and drink with the drunkards, the master of that servant will come on a day when he is not looking for him and at an hour that he is not aware of, and will cut him in two and appoint him his portion with the hypocrites. There shall be weeping and gnashing of teeth.

—Matthew 24:48–51

We see the same warning in the parable of the ten virgins in Matthew 25.

Then the kingdom of heaven shall be likened to ten virgins who took their lamps and went out to meet the bridegroom. Now five of them were wise, and five were foolish. Those who were foolish took their lamps and took no oil with them, but the wise took oil in their vessels with their lamps. But while the bridegroom was delayed, they all slumbered and slept.

And at midnight a cry was heard: "Behold, the bridegroom is coming; go out to meet him!" Then all those virgins arose and trimmed their lamps. And the foolish said to the wise, "Give us some of your oil, for our lamps are going out." But the wise answered, saying, "No, lest there should not be enough for us and you; but go rather to those who sell, and buy for yourselves." And while they went to buy, the bridegroom came, and those who were ready went in with him to the wedding; and the door was shut.

Afterward the other virgins came also, saying, "Lord, Lord, open to us!" But he answered and said, "Assuredly, I say to you, I do not know you." Watch

therefore, for you know neither the day nor the hour
in which the Son of Man is coming.
                                        —MATTHEW 25:1–13

A few years ago God spoke to me and said, "Only a
focus on eternity and the second coming of Christ will
protect my people's minds from the onslaught of the
enemy that is coming." In Laodicea pride, self-sufficiency,
wealth, prosperity, fear of man, and compromise caused
them to become spiritually blind. In other areas of the
church it is a failure to focus on the second coming of
Christ. Whatever the cause of our spiritual blindness, it
is time to cry out to God for spiritual vision. It is time to
repent of every sin, compromise, and distraction that has
come into our lives and cry out to God for eye salve—a
spirit of wisdom and revelation in the deep and intimate
knowledge of God. Believe and receive this gift from God.

As you walk in this new dimension of wisdom and revelation, the Spirit of God is going to open your eyes and
reveal the true nature and character of Jesus. He is also
going to fill your heart and mind with what He is focused
on: the end of the age.

These two things—the focus on the end of the age and
looking unto Jesus—are the keys to overcoming in the end-
time assault. It is time to arise out of our spiritual lukewarmness, pick up our armor, present it back to the Lord so He can
purify it of anything that is not of Him, and begin to march.

This is it. The season of the end of the age has begun. It
might be five years, twenty years, fifty years, or more before
we see it fully manifest, but the end of the age has begun.

CHAPTER 10

THE END OF THE AGE

IN CHAPTER 1 I wrote about the soldiers on the battle-field at the end of the age:

I saw many more soldiers falling away. They would get their eyes off Jesus and be overcome by the dung as it spread all over their bodies until they were totally consumed and fell to the ground. They would then become so covered with dung that they looked as if they had been buried in a shallow grave.

I looked at Jesus as this was happening, and He never flinched or looked back. His focus was straight forward. I thought He was focused on the massive sea of lost humanity, but then I realized He was looking past them. I wondered in my heart what Jesus was looking at.

Then I heard a voice say, "He is focused on the end of the age." I then saw beyond the sea of lost humanity, and there appeared a huge, empty white throne. The thought filled my mind, "Why is it empty? Where's the Father?" I then realized this was Jesus' throne to rule and reign from here on the earth.

Jesus was focused on the end of the age. The phrase "end of the age" is not something I normally would have used. It's not something I am used to hearing. I knew it existed in Scripture, but I never spent much time thinking about it. However, I have found that the phrase is of great importance, and so understanding what it refers to will give us strength in the battles ahead.

> Now as He sat on the Mount of Olives, the disciples came to Him privately, saying, "Tell us, when will these things be? And what will be the sign of Your coming, and of the end of the age?"
> —MATTHEW 24:3

What is the end of the age? Jesus speaks of it as an age to come.

> Anyone who speaks a word against the Son of Man, it will be forgiven him; but whoever speaks against the Holy Spirit, it will not be forgiven him, either in this age or in the age to come.
> —MATTHEW 12:32

> So Jesus answered and said, "Assuredly, I say to you, there is no one who has left house or brothers or sisters or father or mother or wife or children or lands, for My sake and the gospel's, who shall not receive a hundredfold now in this time—houses and brothers and sisters and mothers and children and lands, with persecutions—and in the age to come, eternal life."
> —MARK 10:29–30

There is a time coming soon when the world as we know it will end and a new age—a new period of time—will be ushered in. In this new era Jesus will rule and reign here on earth. This is what Jesus is focused on—returning to the earth, destroying all wickedness, and establishing His millennial reign.

Revelation 19 and 20 give us a glimpse of the period called the end of the age.

> Now I saw heaven opened, and behold, a white horse. And He who sat on him was called Faithful and True, and in righteousness He judges and makes war. His eyes were like a flame of fire, and on His head were many crowns...and His name is called The Word of God. And the armies in heaven...followed Him on white horses. Now out of His mouth goes a sharp sword, that with it He should strike the nations.... And He has on His robe and on His thigh a name written: king of kings and lord of lords.
>
> Then I saw an angel coming down from heaven, having the key to the bottomless pit and a great chain in his hand. He laid hold of the dragon, that serpent of old, who is the Devil and Satan, and bound him for a thousand years; and he cast him into the bottomless pit, and shut him up, and set a seal on him....And I saw thrones, and they sat on them, and judgment was committed to them....And they lived and reigned with Christ for a thousand years....Blessed and holy is he who has part in the first resurrection. Over such the second death has no power, but they shall be priests of God and of Christ, and shall reign with Him a thousand years.
>
> —REVELATION 19:11–16; 20:1–4, 6

There is a lot to unpack in these verses, and I will attempt in this chapter to give a brief overview. First, however, I want to show you why we need to be intensely focused on what Jesus is focused on: the end of the age.

THE HELMET OF SALVATION

Paul writes in Ephesians 6:17, "And take the helmet of salvation." The word salvation in this verse does not speak simply of our born-again experience but rather of our final deliverance. We see this also in 1 Thessalonians 5:8, "But let us who are of the day be sober, putting on the breastplate of faith and love, and as a helmet the hope of salvation." This verse is speaking of the hope of a future, complete deliverance from all the limitations, destructions, weaknesses, sin, suffering, and death of this present age.

This helmet of salvation is the helmet of the hope of salvation—not the hope of being born-again but the hope of our final salvation. It is pointing to the time when we will shed this mortal body, leave the corruptible, and take on the incorruptible. It's the point in time when Jesus comes back and we go to be with Him. It's when we have escaped the limitations of this life, when we've escaped sin, sickness, death, and destruction. It's that time when we will spend all eternity walking by His side, worshipping His name, and forever feasting on the eternal tree of life.

In many modern churches today very little time is spent preaching and teaching on the second coming of Christ and the age to come. This has created a great vulnerability in the church because it disconnects us from the foundation of faith, which is the hope of the age to come.

The Bible tells us, "Now faith is the substance of things

hoped for, the evidence of things not seen" (Heb. 11:1). And Paul wrote, "And now abide faith, hope, love, these three; but the greatest of these is love" (1 Cor. 13:13).

Hope is the foundation of all faith. Hope is a desire with an absolute expectation for fulfillment. Without hope you have no faith. "Faith comes by hearing, and hearing by the word of God" (Rom. 10:7). The preaching of the Word brings the revelation of God and His purposes and produces a hope in the hearts of those who receive the message.

> We give thanks to the God and Father of our Lord Jesus Christ, praying always for you, since we heard of your faith in Christ Jesus and of your love for all the saints; because of the hope which is laid up for you in heaven, of which you heard before in the word of the truth of the gospel.
>
> —COLOSSIANS 1:3–5

The early Christians had faith because they had hope in what was waiting for them in heaven, which they heard about when Paul preached the gospel to them.

> For whatever things were written before were written for our learning, that we through the patience and comfort of the Scriptures might have hope.
>
> —ROMANS 15:4

This may be a shock to hear, but Jesus didn't come preaching mainly on the forgiveness of sin. Scripture says, "From that time Jesus began to preach and to say, 'Repent, for the kingdom of heaven is at hand'" (Matt. 4:17). Jesus spoke often of a new kingdom, a new age, a new period of time when He will rule and reign.

The devil has stolen and perverted the truth of a new

age. The New Age movement is a perversion of the truth. They promise a kind of spiritual utopia on the earth without Jesus. The devil always takes some of the truth and twists it and removes Jesus. You will find that end-time deceptions often promise what Jesus promises but claim you can get it without Jesus. The devil's end-time deception will cause people to believe man can, in and of himself, attain a form of God-likeness.

Jesus told us to pray for this new era to come to the earth when He instructed us to pray, "Your kingdom come. Your will be done on earth as it is in heaven" (Matt. 6:10). Jesus wanted us to pray for the kingdom rule in heaven to be fully established here on earth. Jesus is coming to the earth to rule and reign here. The end of the age is the transition period when Jesus is returning to the earth to judge the nations, destroy the Antichrist, conquer the evil rulers of the world, and establish His holy empire on the earth.

In Old Testament passages referring to Jesus, the Father told Him to ask for the nations of the earth and promised to establish His kingdom forever.

> I will declare the decree: the lord has said to Me, "You are My Son, today I have begotten You. Ask of Me, and I will give You the nations for Your inheritance, and the ends of the earth for Your possession. You shall break them with a rod of iron; You shall dash them to pieces like a potter's vessel."
>
> —Psalm 2:7–9

> I will appoint a place for My people Israel, and will plant them, that they may dwell in a place of their own and move no more; nor shall the sons of

wickedness oppress them anymore....When your days are fulfilled...I will set up your seed after you, who will come from your body [this is referring to Solomon, then eventually Jesus], and I will establish his kingdom....Your house and your kingdom shall be established forever before you. Your throne shall be established forever.

—2 SAMUEL 7:10–12, 16

For unto us a Child is born, unto us a Son is given; and the government will be upon His shoulder. His name will be called Wonderful, Counselor, Mighty God, Everlasting Father, Prince of Peace. Of the increase of His government and peace there will be no end, upon the throne of David and over His kingdom, to order it and establish it with judgment and justice from that time forward, even forever. The zeal of the lord of hosts will perform this.

—ISAIAH 9:6–7

The message of the gospel is not simply that you can avoid hell; it is that the kingdom of heaven is coming to earth. Jesus is coming to take over everything. He is coming in all His glory and power to sit upon His throne in Jerusalem, from which He will judge the nations and reign as the King of kings and Lord of lords.

WE WILL RULE AND REIGN WITH HIM

During a thousand-year period, we will rule and reign with Jesus.

I saw thrones, and they [the saints] sat on them.... And they lived and reigned with Christ for a

thousand years....They shall be priests of God and
of Christ, and shall reign with Him a thousand years.
—REVELATION 20:4–6

This is the hope we are to preach. This is the hope we are
to focus on so we have the faith to endure to the end. In 2016
God gave me a prophetic word for the body of Christ. The
Lord said, "Only a focus on eternity and the return of Christ
will protect you from the mental onslaught of the enemy."

The hope of the victorious King returning to this earth
to destroy everything that hinders love and establish His
throne here will give you great strength to endure till the
end. If you know what the end result will be, you can
endure the suffering that happens on the journey. We
can't afford to merely have head knowledge of this and
believe it mentally. We must have an ever-increasing revelation of the power, glory, and authority of the kingdom
of heaven coming to the earth.

Focusing on what Jesus is focused on gives us the power
and drive to overcome the works of the flesh. When you
have hope, when you have a vision, you have the power to
exercise your will and discipline yourself.

Where there is no revelation, the people cast off
restraint; but happy is he who keeps the law.
—PROVERBS 29:18

When Jesus returns in "the brightness of His coming"
(2 Thess. 2:8) all will see Him as He is. Scripture gives us a
glimpse of what that time will be like both for unbelievers
and believers.

Then the sky receded as a scroll when it is rolled
up, and every mountain and island was moved out

of its place. And the kings of the earth, the great men, the rich men, the commanders, the mighty men, every slave and every free man, hid themselves in the caves and in the rocks of the mountains, and said to the mountains and rocks, "Fall on us and hide us from the face of Him who sits on the throne and from the wrath of the Lamb! For the great day of His wrath has come, and who is able to stand?"

—REVELATION 6:14–17

If then you were raised with Christ, seek those things which are above, where Christ is, sitting at the right hand of God. Set your mind on things above, not on things on the earth. For you died, and your life is hidden with Christ in God. When Christ who is our life appears, then you also will appear with Him in glory.

—COLOSSIANS 3:1–4

This is the hope we have, that Jesus in all His glory is coming back to this world to destroy everything that hinders love. We will all see Him as He is, and when we see Him we shall be like Him. We shall appear with Him in glory.

Without the revelation of who Jesus is and what He is focused on, God's people become unrestrained. The hope of the soon-coming King gives us power to say no to the works of the flesh.

Beloved, now we are children of God; and it has not yet been revealed what we shall be, but we know that when He is revealed, we shall be like Him, for we shall see Him as He is. And everyone

who has this hope in Him purifies himself, just as
He is pure.

—1 JOHN 3:2–3

With our focus on Jesus and His appearing at the end of the age, Paul tell us to

> put to death your members which are on the earth:
> fornication, uncleanness, passion, evil desire, and cov-
> etousness, which is idolatry. Because of these things
> the wrath of God is coming upon the sons of disobe-
> dience, in which you yourselves once walked when
> you lived in them. But now you yourselves are to put
> off all these: anger, wrath, malice, blasphemy, filthy
> language out of your mouth. Do not lie to one another,
> since you have put off the old man with his deeds, and
> have put on the new man who is renewed in knowl-
> edge according to the image of Him who created him.
>
> —COLOSSIANS 3:5–10

Everyone who has an active, progressive revelation of the hope of Christ's return, our being with Him in glory, and our being transfigured into His image purifies himself from the works of the flesh.

Hope in the glorious second coming of Christ to rule and reign on earth is the foundation of the faith you will need to endure till the end. This hope is an amazing weapon against shame because shame always causes you to focus on yourself. It causes you to flee the presence of God, make excuses, blame others, and ultimately blame God. Shame will keep you from being able to believe and accept the glorious future you have with Jesus when He returns.

The enemy will use shame in these last days to manip-ulate people to compromise the gospel and reject the true working of the Spirit of God. Shame robs us of hope, and hope breaks the power of shame.

> Therefore, since we have been justified by faith, we have peace with God through our Lord Jesus Christ. Through him we have also obtained access by faith into this grace in which we stand, and we rejoice in hope of the glory of God. Not only that, but we rejoice in our sufferings, knowing that suffering produces endurance, and endurance produces character, and character produces hope, and *hope does not put us to shame*, because God's love has been poured into our hearts through the Holy Spirit who has been given to us.
> —ROMANS 5:1–5, ESV, EMPHASIS ADDED

Hope does not put us to shame. So even though we may be suffering from persecutions, temptations, false accusations, tribulations, and the shaming of the world, the hope of the glory of God "never disappoints or deludes or shames us" (Rom. 5:5, AMPC).

Paul said, "This is in keeping with my own eager desire and persistent expectation and hope, that I shall not disgrace myself nor be put to shame in anything; but that with the utmost freedom of speech and unfailing courage, now as always heretofore, Christ (the Messiah) will be magnified and get glory and praise in this body of mine and be boldly exalted in my person, whether through (by) life or through (by) death" (Phil. 1:20, AMPC). Hope, which frees us from shame, will produce in us "the utmost freedom of speech and unfailing courage, now as always heretofore."

The days we are entering into are going to be the most challenging mankind has ever experienced. The enemy is going to attack the church with an onslaught of the works of the flesh and religious persecution. Shame will be one of the devil's greatest end-time weapons. There will be an unrelenting assault by the spirit of shame. "Yet if anyone suffers as a Christian, let him not be ashamed, but let him glorify God in this matter" (1 Pet. 4:16).

And "since Christ suffered for us in the flesh, arm yourselves also with the same mind, for he who has suffered in the flesh has ceased from sin, that he no longer should live the rest of his time in the flesh for the lusts of men, but for the will of God" (1 Pet. 4:1–2).

The devil will try to shame you for your failures. The world will try to shame you for your faith. The enemy will try to shame you for suffering. But Jesus bore your shame.

Again, we must look "unto Jesus, the author and finisher of our faith, who for the joy that was set before Him endured the cross, despising the shame, and has sat down at the right hand of the throne of God. For consider Him who endured such hostility from sinners against Himself, lest you become weary and discouraged in your souls" (Heb. 12:2–3).

The mystery of the gospel is "Christ in you, the hope of glory" (Col. 1:27). "When Christ who is our life appears, then you also will appear with Him in glory" (Col. 3:4). Keeping your eyes focused on Jesus and what He is focused on—the end of the age—will cancel the noise of shame.

PART IV

THE KEYS TO DEFEATING SHAME

CHAPTER 11

CHOSEN BEFORE
THE FOUNDATION
OF THE WORLD

I N THE EARLY 2000s I went to Seoul, South Korea, for the first time to minister. The journey there was rough. I was traveling there from the Philippines, where I had been for two weeks, and on the last night of my time in the Philippines I was awakened at midnight by a strange sound.

When I turned on the lights, the entire back wall of my room was covered with hundreds of thousands of termites. The place where I was staying had no food available, and the host forgot to arrange for someone to bring me something to eat, so I hadn't eaten for some time, and now my room was being invaded by insects.

I called the front desk, and they moved me to another room, but when I opened the door and turned on the lights hundreds of cockroaches fled in every direction. I was moved to a third room, where only a few dozen cockroaches fled. As you might imagine, I didn't sleep well.

My plane to South Korea was a two-hour drive away, and we were supposed to leave at 6 a.m., but the driver didn't show up until seven. We got stuck for an hour behind a road construction crew, then we got a flat tire. With no time to get a bite to eat, we rushed to the airport only to find the flight had just been closed. I begged the flight attendant to let me on the flight, and thankfully I was allowed to board.

It was a five-hour flight, so I thought I could get some food on the plane. The plane was packed, and I was exactly in the middle. When the flight attendant got to me she apologized that they had run out of food. So here I was, hungry, tired, stressed, and looking forward to my hotel room and some food in Seoul.

I was being picked up by the event coordinator, whom I had never met. I always give instructions for the person picking me up from the airport to have a sign with my name on it so we can easily find each other. When I arrived in Seoul, exited customs, and made my way into the arrival lounge, I looked for someone holding a sign with my name but saw no one. I searched and searched for an hour. I had not been given a contact number, so I had no way of getting ahold of the person picking me up. After an hour I started going from person to person asking if they were looking for Steve Foss.

Finally a woman responded, "Yes. You don't look like him." I said, "Where is your sign with my name?" She said, "I had seen your picture and was sure I would recognize you."

In my picture I was wearing a nice suit. I travel in jeans

and a T-shirt. She looked at my clothes and said, "Where is your suit?" I told her, "In my garment bag." She said with a sense of urgency, "Quickly, put it on; we have meeting in big church." I replied, "First take me to my hotel, and I will quickly change. My suit will be wrinkled, and I need to iron it." She said, "No time. You go to bathroom and put it on." My protest didn't work, as she was very insistent.

I went to the airport bathroom and put on my wrinkled suit, and we proceeded to ride a cramped city bus into town. As we rounded the corner an hour later, she proclaimed, "There it is; there's the church." My heart sank as I recognized the church building. It was Yoido Full Gospel Church, the largest church in the world. I was hungry, stressed, tired, and wearing a wrinkled suit, and now I was about to preach at the largest church in the world. This visit was not going well.

The woman tried to contact the host pastor but couldn't get through. We stood outside the building for some time waiting. We ended up being too late and missed the service, and all of this happened because she thought she knew what I looked like. She had an image in her mind of me that wasn't what I really looked like. Because of her failure to recognize me as I am, problems ensued. Fortunately, by the grace of God I was able to preach there twice later in the trip.

You may have guessed my point: we need to see Jesus as He is, not as we think He is. The image you have of Jesus will determine how you respond to Him. When John was having the vision of Jesus that became the Book of Revelation, he first heard a voice. He turned in the direction of the sound, and this is how he described what he saw.

> And having turned I saw seven golden lampstands, and in the midst of the seven lampstands One like the Son of Man, clothed with a garment down to the feet and girded about the chest with a golden band. His head and hair were white like wool, as white as snow, and His eyes like a flame of fire; His feet were like fine brass, as if refined in a furnace, and His voice as the sound of many waters; He had in His right hand seven stars, out of His mouth went a sharp two-edged sword, and His countenance was like the sun shining in its strength. And when I saw Him, I fell at His feet as dead. But He laid His right hand on me, saying to me, "Do not be afraid; I am the First and the Last."
>
> —Revelation 1:12–17

Can you imagine how powerful this vision must have been for John to be so overwhelmed that he fell to the ground as one dead? This is the same John who walked with Jesus for three years. He is the same John who saw all the miracles, heard the preaching, saw Jesus transfigured on top of the mountain, saw Moses and Elijah, saw Jesus after He had been raised from the dead, and saw Him ascend into heaven in a cloud. And yet this vision of Jesus was so far beyond anything he had ever seen or experienced that he fell to the ground as though dead.

No matter how many encounters you have had with the Lord before—and I doubt they are anywhere near what John had—you have only ever seen a glimpse of what He wants to reveal to you. Each of the descriptions of Jesus in Revelation 1–3 are so powerful and life-changing that I'm going to devote an entire book to them. But in this chapter I want to focus on His eyes of fire.

> His head and hair were white like wool, as white as
> snow, and His eyes like a flame of fire.
>
> —REVELATION 1:14

Many people might think this verse reveals Jesus as an angry, fierce God coming with judgment because we tend to equate fire with judgment, suffering, and destruction. However, this description is so much more than that and far more glorious. When we discover what these amazing eyes of fire reveal about the heart and passion of Jesus, it will change our relationship with Him forever.

God's eyes of fire see everything. There is nothing hidden from God's sight. King David declared:

> O Lord, you have examined my heart and know
> everything about me. You know when I sit down or
> stand up. You know my thoughts even when I'm far
> away. You see me when I travel and when I rest at
> home. You know everything I do. You know what I
> am going to say even before I say it, LORD.
>
> —PSALM 139:1–4, NLT

The revelation that God is present everywhere and sees all is both comforting and terrifying. There is nowhere we can hide from God or be hidden from Him. God's eyes of fire see everything.

Fire doesn't emanate just from His eyes; God is surrounded by fire.

> I watched till thrones were put in place, and the
> Ancient of Days was seated; His garment was white
> as snow, and the hair of His head was like pure wool.
> His throne was a fiery flame, its wheels a burning
> fire; a fiery stream issued and came forth from

before Him. A thousand thousands ministered to Him; ten thousand times ten thousand stood before Him. The court was seated, and the books were opened.

—DANIEL 7:9–10

John answered, saying to all, "I indeed baptize you with water; but One mightier than I is coming, whose sandal strap I am not worthy to loose. He will baptize you with the Holy Spirit and fire. His winnowing fan is in His hand, and He will thoroughly clean out His threshing floor, and gather the wheat into His barn; but the chaff He will burn with unquenchable fire."

—LUKE 3:16–17

The image of God surrounded by fire and fire proceeding from His throne reveals three incredible truths about God and His interaction with mankind: that He has passionate, fiery love for us; He is a purifying fire; and we cannot avoid the fire of His judgment.

THE FIRE OF GOD'S PASSIONATE DESIRE

Those piercing eyes are first and foremost eyes filled with passionate desire. It is difficult for many to truly see God as passionate, emotional, and even consumed with desire for someone. But God's desire for us is as a consuming fire.

Deuteronomy 4:24 says, "For the Lord your God is a consuming fire, a jealous God." Our God is a jealous God. This heavenly jealousy is an all-consuming fire. This is not a worldly jealousy; it is an all-consuming love for us that causes God to want and demand every part of our being. He so desires you that He wants *every part* of you.

Nothing is to be held back from Him. His love for you is so complete, so total, so irreversible that it is as a fire.

Because the fire of His holy desire for us is all-consuming, it requires judgment against all that hinders us from entering into this love relationship. God doesn't bring judgment because He is a mean, temperamental, vengeful God. He brings judgment to remove everything that hinders the manifestation of His holy fire of love and desire for us.

The Father foreordained mankind to become a holy, spotless bride for His Son. He created us to experience the highest level of intimacy and oneness with Him. This is what He had in mind for us before the foundation of the world. Mankind is unique to all of God's creations. We were created in the image of God, unlike the angels, the cherubim, and the living creatures. We were created not just to be God's children but to be one with Christ as Jesus' bride.

> For we are members of His body, of His flesh and of His bones. "For this reason a man shall leave his father and mother and be joined to his wife, and the two shall become one flesh." This is a great mystery, but I speak concerning Christ and the church.
>
> —EPHESIANS 5:30–32

God chose you for Himself. He didn't create and love you just as another one of His creations. He formed you and me for one great and glorious reason—that we may be joined together with God and filled with the Godhead.

> For in Him the whole fullness of Deity (the Godhead) continues to dwell in bodily form [giving complete expression of the divine nature]. And you

are in Him, made full and having come to fullness of
life [in Christ you too are filled with the Godhead—
Father, Son and Holy Spirit—and reach full spiritual
stature]. And He is the Head of all rule and authority
[of every angelic principality and power].

—Colossians 2:9–10, AMPC

The truth that you and I were created for a higher purpose—to experience intimacy and oneness with God as
the bride of Christ—makes us unique among all His creation and gives us insight into the intensity of God's eyes
of fiery desire for us. He chose us for this glorious eternal
purpose before the world began.

Even as [in His love] He chose us [actually picked
us out for Himself as His own] in Christ before the
foundation of the world, that we should be holy
(consecrated and set apart for Him) and blameless in
His sight, even above reproach, before Him in love.

—Ephesians 1:4, AMPC

CHOSEN IN HIM

The first and probably most foundational weapon against
the curse of shame is to see that God has eyes of fiery love
for you. This desire has never been dependent upon your
works, for He chose you before you were even born. He
made up His mind about you before the foundation of the
world. You have been "predestined to be conformed to the
image of His Son" (Rom. 8:29).

Let this sink deep into your spirit: God, through His
foreknowledge, chose you and me before the foundation
of the world that we should be made holy, blameless, pure,
and conformed into the exact image of Jesus Christ.

God "has saved us and called us with a holy calling, not according to our works, but according to His own purpose and grace which was given to us in Christ Jesus before time began" (2 Tim. 1:9). He chose us before time began for His purposes and His good pleasure. This point is critical in helping us get our eyes off ourselves and on Him.

There is a lot of good teaching about God's love toward us. We sing songs about how much God loves us and the fact that we're His children. These songs are great, but they tend to obscure one of the great truths that will deliver us from the curse of shame.

The intensity of God's fiery desire for us is amplified because of our eternal purpose, which is to be the bride of Christ. The depth of God's love for us exceeds even His love for us as individuals because of the eternal purpose for which we were created. Put another way, God's love for me is not simply because of me and it's not exclusively for me. The Father loves me because I am part of His redemptive plan to prepare a bride for His Son, Jesus, who is the only One worthy to receive the fullness of the Father's love. The Father's all-consuming, fiery desire for us is an extension of His love for His Son.

Why would God be willing to send His Son to redeem mankind but not to redeem fallen angels? The devil and his angels only have a future in the lake of fire, but God has made a way for us to spend eternity with Him as the bride of Christ. There is something different about us. We were created for a different purpose. We were created for Jesus.

God didn't create you, forgive you, save you, or even love you for your pleasure but for His good pleasure.

Thou art worthy, O Lord, to receive glory and honor and power: for thou hast created all things, and for thy pleasure they are and were created.

—REVELATION 4:11, KJV

Blessed be the God and Father of our Lord Jesus Christ, who has blessed us with every spiritual blessing in the heavenly places in Christ, just as He chose us in Him before the foundation of the world, that we should be holy and without blame before Him in love, having predestined us to adoption as sons by Jesus Christ to Himself, according to the good pleasure of His will, to the praise of the glory of His grace, by which He made us accepted in the Beloved...having made known to us the mystery of His will, according to His good pleasure which He purposed in Himself.

—EPHESIANS 1:3–6, 9

God has revealed His eternal plan to us according to His good pleasure. We were created for God, for His praise and for His glory. We were created for Him. This shift in focus is key to walking free from shame. We must get our eyes off ourselves and our current circumstances and onto the eternal plan of God. We were not born simply so we could be happy and have a nice life, good marriage, and healthy kids. We were created for God's good pleasure, plans, purposes, and will.

Lucifer's fall began when he started to focus on himself. The key to walking free from all the strategies of Satan is to keep our eyes off ourselves. Again, God didn't create me for my pleasure and enjoyment. God made me for His good pleasure. I am on this earth forgiven, blessed, filled, and healed to fulfill His plans and purposes, not mine. As Paul wrote, "For by Him all things were created that are in heaven and that are on earth, visible and invisible, whether thrones or dominions or principalities or powers. All things were created through Him and for Him" (Col. 1:16).

ALL THINGS WERE CREATED FOR HIM

The real power of the revelation of God's love comes when we see the motive of God's love. As long as we see God's fiery desire for us through the lens of how it benefits us, we are prone to the lies of shame that cause us to withdraw from God. We start hearing lies in our head such as, "How can God love me? Look how much I messed up. I'm not worthy; I'm not good enough; I'm not strong enough." And on and on the lies go.

As long as we keep focusing on ourselves, whether positively or negatively, we are prone to fall into Satan's traps. We must keep looking unto Jesus. God loves us because of and for His good pleasure, will, plan, and eternal purpose, not because of how good or worthy we are. Only Jesus is worthy.

This is a hard concept for some to grasp because our entire culture is me-centered. Our social media pages are all about us, our opinions, what we're doing, the meals we ate, where we're going, and the like. We post our updates and get offended if they aren't liked by enough people. "Look at me" is the cry.

In 1988 I was praying in our church sanctuary, preparing for our Friday youth service. I was going to preach on the fear of God. I would generally spend three hours in prayer before I preached. After about two hours I had an amazing encounter with the Lord that underscores this point. I was kneeling facing backward in one of the pews when I sensed the presence of the Lord directly in front of me. I didn't see Him with my natural eyes, but I knew He was there.

I became overwhelmed by the intensity of this manifestation of God. The fear of the Lord flooded my heart for the next hour. I started to confess sins I never even knew were sins. I wept, shook, confessed, repented, and felt laid bare before God.

I didn't hear the Father speak to me until the end of this hour, and what He said changed my life. He said, "Son, everything I do, I never do it for you, because you are not worthy. Everything I do I do for My Son, Jesus, for only Jesus is worthy. I do these things toward you, but I do it for Him."

Everything God does—the blessings, mercy, forgiveness, provision, healing, and so much more—He does because of and for Jesus, not because of or for you and me. There is only One who is worthy to receive anything, and His name is Jesus.

> Then I saw a strong angel proclaiming with a loud voice, "Who is worthy to open the scroll and to loose its seals?" And no one in heaven or on the earth or under the earth was able to open the scroll, or to look at it. So I wept much, because no one was found worthy to open and read the scroll, or to look at it. But one of the elders said to me, "Do not weep. Behold, the Lion of the tribe of Judah, the Root of David, has prevailed to open the scroll and to loose its seven seals."
>
> And I looked, and behold, in the midst of the throne and of the four living creatures, and in the midst of the elders, stood a Lamb as though it

had been slain, having seven horns and seven eyes, which are the seven Spirits of God sent out into all the earth. Then He came and took the scroll out of the right hand of Him who sat on the throne. Now when He had taken the scroll, the four living creatures and the twenty-four elders fell down before the Lamb, each having a harp, and golden bowls full of incense, which are the prayers of the saints. And they sang a new song, saying: "You are worthy to take the scroll, and to open its seals; for You were slain, and have redeemed us to God by Your blood out of every tribe and tongue and people and nation, and have made us kings and priests to our God; and we shall reign on the earth."

—Revelation 5:2–10

The Father loves the Son and has given all things into His hand (John 3:35). The Father gave mankind to Jesus because He loved Jesus and foreordained mankind to be the bride of Christ. Jesus loves the Father and will do the will of the Father above all things to bring Him pleasure. Jesus loves us with the same love with which He loves the Father because the Father chose us in Him before the foundation of the world to be the bride of Christ.

Let me put it this way. Jesus loves you not just because of you but because you were specifically chosen by His Father to be His precious, eternal bride. When someone of great importance gives you a gift, you often love the gift not so much for what it is but because of who gave it to you. Jesus' love for you is so complete and unshakable because the Father gave you to Him. His love for you is more about the fact that the Father created you and gave you to Him as a gift; it is not mainly driven by how good you are in your own eyes or the eyes of others.

When I was about twelve I had a huge misunderstanding with my stepmother. That year for Christmas she and my dad paid for me, my three brothers, and my mother to spend a week at Disney World. It was a huge gift, and I remember being filled with joy and excitement when they told us. I tried to thank my stepmother but said it in a way that she misunderstood. I'd had a tough relationship with her up to that point and felt very insecure around her. Instead of affirming my gratitude, she got upset and we got into a huge fight. I ran to a bedroom and cried and told my dad, "I hate her." After some time she came into the room and apologized when she understood that I was trying to thank her.

In an act of kindness my stepmother gave me a nice throw pillow that night. I kept that pillow for many years, not because it was a great pillow but because my step-mother gave it to me as an act of love. It didn't matter how smelly, torn, old, and dirty it became over time. I loved that pillow because of who gave it to me and why. That pillow always reminded me of her love and forgiveness. Because it was given to me out of love, it had far greater value to me than another pillow would.

Jesus loves us far more than we deserve because we are the Father's gift to Him. So no matter how torn, dirty, smelly, or old we get, He loves us because of who gave us to Him.

Now with this in perspective we can begin to look deeply at the incredible, fiery desire God has for us.

> You have ravished my heart, my sister, my spouse;
> you have ravished my heart with one look of your
> eyes, with one link of your necklace.
>
> —SONG OF SOLOMON 4:9

The love story told in Song of Solomon, which represents Jesus and His bride, powerfully reveals the depth of Jesus' love and delight in us. The bridegroom in the Song of Solomon said it took only one look and His heart was ravished. Jesus' heart is ravished every time we look to Him. Every time we acknowledge Him, lift our voice in prayer or worship, or just stop to gaze upon Him, we ravish His heart.

The word *ravished* means "to overcome with emotion (such as joy or delight)";[1] "to fill (someone) with intense delight; enrapture."[2] "A summary of the Hebrew definition and its English equivalent of the word 'ravished' is *to overwhelm with emotions of delight because of one who is unusually beautiful, attractive, pleasing, or striking.*"[3]

Can you imagine Jesus overwhelmed with delight simply when you look to Him? Jesus passionately desires you and wants you to be with Him where He is. (See John 17:24.)

Jesus looks at you with eyes of fiery desire because the Father chose you for Him before the foundations of the earth. Jesus loves you with the same love with which the Father loves Him. Think about that for a moment. God loves you to the same degree that God loves God.

> I in them, and You in Me; that they may be made
> perfect in one, and that the world may know that
> You have sent Me, and have loved them as You have
> loved Me.
>
> —JOHN 17:23

Jesus loves us the way the Father loves Jesus. God loves us the way God loves God. And now because we, the chosen, have responded to the call, Jesus begins to reveal Himself for a divine purpose.

> And I have declared to them Your name, and will declare it, that the love with which You loved Me may be in them, and I in them.
>
> —JOHN 17:26

God's name speaks of His nature, character, and authority. Jesus says in essence, "I will continue to declare (reveal) Your nature, character, and authority to them, that the same love that You have had for Me for all time may be in them. I want My chosen to experience the fire of My holy love." This is why He sent the Holy Spirit.

> Such hope never disappoints or deludes or shames us, for God's love has been poured out in our hearts through the Holy Spirit Who has been given to us.
>
> —ROMANS 5:5, AMPC

God's jealous love for us is so intense that it manifests itself in and through His righteous judgments. Because He so longs to fill every part of us with Himself, "the Lord disciplines those He loves, and He punishes each one He accepts as His child" (Heb. 12:6). The Lord, with His eyes of fiery desire, purges us of all that hinders us from fully experiencing His *agape* love.

You were chosen, but you were not simply chosen to escape hell. You were chosen to become like Jesus. The work of redemption was not to get you out of hell or even into heaven; it was to get you to Him.

For whom He foreknew, He also predestined to be conformed to the image of His Son, that He might be the firstborn among many brethren. Moreover whom He predestined, these He also called; whom He called, these He also justified; and whom He justified, these He also glorified.

—Romans 8:29–30

Blessed be the God and Father of our Lord Jesus Christ, who has blessed us with every spiritual blessing in the heavenly places in Christ, just as He chose us in Him before the foundation of the world, that we should be holy and without blame before Him in love, having predestined us to adoption as sons by Jesus Christ to Himself.

—Ephesians 1:3–5

HIS FIERY DESIRE PRODUCES HOLINESS IN US

God's love is not separate from His holiness; it is a full manifestation of His holiness. Sin separates us from God. His intense, fiery desire for us is accompanied by His working in us His righteousness. This is not just in a positional sense, where we say we are holy because of the blood. We are able to say, "Because of the blood, I'm actually starting to live holy."

His eyes of fire are on us; He sees all.

His eyes of fire are focused on us. He passionately desires us.

His eyes of fire are against all that hinders love. He will chasten us so we can walk in the fullness of His love. His eyes penetrate all.

> For the Word that God speaks is alive and full of power [making it active, operative, energizing, and effective]; it is sharper than any two-edged sword, penetrating to the dividing line of the breath of life (soul) and [the immortal] spirit, and of joints and marrow [of the deepest parts of our nature], exposing and sifting and analyzing and judging the very thoughts and purposes of the heart. And not a creature exists that is concealed from His sight, but all things are open and exposed, naked and defenseless to the eyes of Him with Whom we have to do.
> —HEBREWS 4:12–13, AMPC

Jesus' fire of desire creates the need for Him to bring judgment. Judgment doesn't always mean punishment. Judgment is the process through which God establishes His verdict. In those of us who are believers responding to God's love, God will expose the areas of sin and disobedience in our lives so we can humbly repent and yield them to Him at the cross. Those of us who truly want to be close to God will ask Him for His judgments like the psalmist who declared, "My soul breaks with longing for Your judgments at all times" (Ps. 119:20).

God is holy, righteous, just, merciful, loving, kind, longsuffering, fierce, and full of wisdom and truth all at the same time. If you are truly seeking to know Him, you must be willing to allow the eyes of His fiery desire to expose you. You must be willing to let Him purge you of the lies, sins, rebellions, and deceptions that are in your heart so you can truly be free.

When we let the eyes of fire that are so filled with His love, mercy, and passion for us expose the deepest secrets of our hearts, we are not filled with shame but truth. Our heart cry becomes, "Search me, O God, and know my heart: try me, and know my thoughts: and see if there be any wicked way in me, and lead me in the way everlasting" (Ps. 139:23–24).

When our eyes are not looking unto Jesus and beholding His eyes of fiery desire for us, our relationship with God will be influenced by outside traffic, noise, and distractions, and we will spend our time and energy jockeying for position and seeking the approval of men. When we seek man's approval we are vulnerable to the weapon of shame. Our sense of approval and acceptance must be rooted in His desire for and enjoyment of us.

Only as we allow the fire of His desire for us to flood our souls will we stop caring about what others think of us. While on the cross Jesus was able to despise the shame (meaning He thought so little of it that it had no power to influence His behavior) because He understood the Father's passionate love for Him. Jesus came to do the Father's will, which was to redeem you and me for Himself. Jesus was able to defeat shame because of the intensity of the Father's love for Him and His love for the Father's gift to Him: His bride, the church.

We must come to the realization that He chose us before the foundation of the world and passionately desires us. Jesus' eyes of fiery desire are turned toward us. He delights in us, even when we are weak and have failed, because we are a gift from the Father.

The truth that we are chosen in Him is one of three main revelations of Jesus we need to know to defeat the curse of shame. We must also understand that we are covered by His righteousness, as we will discover in the next chapter, and crowned with glory and honor.

CHAPTER 12

COVERED WITH THE ROBE OF RIGHTEOUSNESS

J OHN WROTE IN Revelation 3:18, "I counsel you to buy from Me...white garments, that you may be clothed, that the shame of your nakedness may not be revealed." The most painful part of shame is the feeling of being naked and exposed. It brings a feeling of vulnerability, so we are desperate to cover or remove our shame. Only the revelation of Jesus can truly cover and remove our shame.

The concept of covering goes all the way back to the garden. When Adam and Eve sinned and saw they were naked, shame filled them and they grabbed fig leaves to cover themselves. Then when they heard the voice of the Lord in the garden, they were filled with fear and tried to cover their nakedness with another layer by hiding from God among the trees.

> Then the LORD God called to Adam and said to him,
> "Where are you?" So he said, "I heard Your voice in
> the garden, and I was afraid because I was naked;
> and I hid myself." And He said, "Who told you that
> you were naked? Have you eaten from the tree of
> which I commanded you that you should not eat?"
> —GENESIS 3:9–11

The Father began to question Adam and asked, "Who told you that you were naked?" In other words, "Who told you to be ashamed?" God was going to the root of the problem, which was their disobedience. Adam, filled with shame, then resorted to a third way of trying to cover his shame. He shifted the blame.

> Then the man said, "The woman whom You gave to
> be with me, she gave me of the tree, and I ate."
> —GENESIS 3:12

Not only did Adam blame the woman; he blamed God. Adam said, "The woman whom *You* gave me..." In other words, "It's really Your fault, God. I wouldn't have sinned and be filled with shame had You not given me the woman."

Ever since the garden mankind has been doing the same three things to try to cover his shame.

1. SEWING FIG LEAVES

First we sew "fig leaves," trying to make up for our sin and cover our shame with our own efforts. We use clothing, wealth, popularity, education, physical appearance, and so much more to try to cover our shame. We also try to pay a price, whether it is to beat ourselves up and/or submit to societal punishments, so we can redeem ourselves.

The fig leaves represent mankind trying to do good works to make up for our "sins." I placed *sins* in quotes because not everything we are made to feel ashamed of is a true sin. There are real sins we commit, and there are sins people accuse us of and things society has declared sinful. An example is seen in the anti-racist movement today. We are told it's not good enough just to condemn racism; we must prove, through an ever-changing series of public actions, that we are anti-racist.

The claim is that White people are inherently racist and therefore must prove they're not racist by doing, saying, and acting in ways that the anti-racist leaders define. The purveyors of anti-racism, and so many other ungodly philosophies, say this is the only way you can truly remove the shame of your White ancestors' complicity in racism throughout American history, absolve yourself of your own inherent racism, and prove your "righteousness." This is not only demonic, it is the antithesis of Christ's work on the cross. Works of the flesh don't change hearts or make a person righteous. Only the blood of Jesus can forgive and remove sin, and only the robe of righteousness can cover our shame and present us righteous before God.

2. HIDING FROM GOD

Second, Adam and Eve hid themselves from the presence of God. This happens both inside and outside the church. When shame comes, especially from sins we commit as opposed to things we're falsely accused of, we run away from God's presence. We try to hide from the voice of the Lord in the Spirit of the day.

In other words, we try to find a way to not face the truth

of God's Word. This is accomplished many ways. Inside the church we stop preaching on certain scriptures. We no longer use words such as *repent, sin, hell,* or *judgment.* We present a Jesus who accepts people unconditionally because we equate unconditional love with unconditional acceptance, and they are not the same.

Just because God loves you doesn't mean He is required to accept whatever you do. We see this played out in the LGBTQ community. A child raised in a Christian family comes home to tell his Christian parents, "I'm gay. God loves me and made me this way, and if you love me, you will accept me as I am." He has just used the weapon of shame. What he is really saying is, "I have rejected God's authority to tell me homosexuality is a sin. I am yielding to this work of the flesh. If you don't accept me, then you really don't love me. Shame on you."

So what have many Christian parents done? They have fallen prey to this trap because they wrongly think unconditional love and unconditional acceptance are one and the same. They are not. God unconditionally loved the world so much that He gave His only begotten Son. However, God will also judge the wicked. Unless we repent of and abandon our sins, we will not enter the kingdom of heaven.

God doesn't accept you unconditionally. You must confess with your mouth the Lord Jesus and believe in your heart that God raised Him from the dead. If you continue in your sin, the Scriptures are clear.

> For this you know, that no fornicator, unclean person, nor covetous man, who is an idolater, has any inheritance in the kingdom of Christ and God. Let no one deceive you with empty words, for

because of these things the wrath of God comes upon the sons of disobedience. Therefore do not be partakers with them.

—EPHESIANS 5:5–7

Do you not know that the unrighteous will not inherit the kingdom of God? Do not be deceived. Neither fornicators, nor idolaters, nor adulterers, nor homosexuals, nor sodomites, nor thieves, nor covetous, nor drunkards, nor revilers, nor extortioners will inherit the kingdom of God. And such were some of you. But you were washed, but you were sanctified, but you were justified in the name of the Lord Jesus and by the Spirit of our God.

—1 CORINTHIANS 6:9–11

No matter how much you love your children you can never reject the truth of God's Word. Often parents who do this are simply trying to avoid shame. In the previous example the parents who accept their child's conditions are trying to escape the shame by failing to speak the truth in love and call their son to repentance. The homosexual child is doing the same thing in a different way. He is trying to deal with his shame by hiding from the Word of God and denying its truth and authority over his life.

The unsaved and the world are constantly trying to hide from the voice of the Lord by rejecting the Bible in society, mocking the preachers of righteousness, legislating and legalizing immorality, and canceling Christians who stand for righteousness. These and many more actions are man's efforts to hide from the shame of their wickedness.

3. BLAMING OTHERS

Third, they blame others and then ultimately God. In the example about the family dealing with homosexuality, the son claimed falsely that God made him that way. "It's not my fault I'm living a homosexual lifestyle," he says. "God made me this way." This is a classic example of blame shifting.

"I wouldn't be this way if God hadn't allowed me to be abused, if God had given me a better father, or if God had made me part of a different race, culture, or economic status," they say in their hearts. "God, You made me this way, so it's Your fault I have done what I have done; therefore, I don't need to feel ashamed. How dare You judge me since it's really Your fault." Trying to cover our shame with our own works, denying God's Word and running from His presence, or blaming others and God will never truly deliver us from the curse of shame.

The amazing attributes of Jesus revealed in Revelation chapters 1–3 continue to bring us freedom from the lies and shame of the enemy. Although each of these principles gives us power over shame in any form it comes, the primary way we walk free from shame is to take our actual sins, failures, and weaknesses to God.

> To Him who loved us and washed us from our sins in His own blood, and has made us kings and priests to His God and Father, to Him be glory and dominion forever and ever. Amen.
> —REVELATION 1:5–6

This verse encapsulates the three keys to overcoming shame.

1. We are chosen—He "loved us."

2. We are covered—He "washed us from our
   sins in His own blood."

3. We are crowned—He "has made us kings
   and priests to His God and Father."

We've looked at the fact that we are chosen. Let us now look at being covered. Man tried to cover his own shame, but from the beginning the Lord began to point to Jesus, who was the only One who could take our sins away. In the Old Testament the people of Israel shed the blood of innocent lambs to atone for and cover their sins. It was a temporary withholding of God's righteous judgment until Jesus came.

Jesus came not only to forgive us of our sin but also to deliver us from our sin nature. When Adam and Eve fell, sin entered the world. A new nature was born inside of Adam: a sin nature, or what some would call a carnal nature. It is that fallen human nature which causes us to reject God's legal authority over our lives.

Jesus came not only to forgive us but also to deliver us from this sin nature so we can truly walk free. Jesus declared, "Therefore if the Son makes you free, you shall be free indeed" (John 8:36). The Book of Romans spends much time addressing this issue. Romans 3:20–5:11 speaks of the blood of Jesus being applied to the actual sins we commit.

> Blessed are those whose lawless deeds are forgiven,
> and whose sins are covered; blessed is the man to
> whom the Lord shall not impute sin.
>
> —ROMANS 4:7–8

The blood of Jesus has paid the price for our sins and covered us in His righteousness. The realization of our forgiveness is foundational to our relationship with Christ. However, many who believe they are forgiven still struggle with shame. To try to deal with this shame we teach and preach more and more on God's grace, mercy, and forgiveness. Some even try to convince people that since they are Christians their sin doesn't count anymore so they shouldn't worry about it. The focus often seems to be on finding ways to alleviate the pain of the shame. "Don't worry, be happy" is the mantra. God's got you covered; sin doesn't exist for Christians, some falsely claim. Books on who we are in Christ, the authority of the believer, and our covenant with God are pushed. We're told to pray harder, fast more, give more, serve, and sing songs about being a friend of God's. And our frail attempts to remove the pain of shame continue.

Yet no matter how many sermons we listen to, prayers we confess, and songs we sing, the shame doesn't go away. There is value in many of these things, but they never seem to be enough. So much of the body of Christ still deals with the torment of shame. As long as we are focused on ourselves we will never truly be free. *Our focus must be on His righteousness.*

WE ARE COVERED WITH HIS RIGHTEOUSNESS

I will greatly rejoice in the LORD, my soul shall be joyful in my God; for He has clothed me with the garments of salvation, He has covered me with the robe of righteousness.

—ISAIAH 61:10

I particularly love the image of a robe of righteousness in this verse from Isaiah. It is not just any robe; it is the kingly robe of Jesus. The idea is not just covering our filth and shame but clothing us with a royal garment. The kingly robe of righteousness beautifies us and establishes our heavenly position. It is a robe that declares to the universe that we are the chosen, precious sons and daughters of God. We are kings and priests of the Most High; we are royalty.

> For He made Him who knew no sin to be sin for us,
> that we might become the righteousness of God in
> Him.
>
> —2 Corinthians 5:21

One of the descriptions of Jesus found in Hebrews 7:2 is King of righteousness. The common definition for righteousness you will hear from many preachers is to be in right standing with God. The thought is that because our sins are forgiven, we are now in right relationship with God. This is a powerful truth, yet it falls far short of the amazing revelation of what righteousness truly is and why Jesus' title as the King of righteousness is such a powerful weapon against the curse of shame.

The word *righteousness* comes from the Greek term *dikaios*, which is translated "righteous," "right," or "just."[1] The word speaks of a total conformity to the character and nature of God, "the act of doing what is required according to a standard."[2] The term *judgment*, or *justice*, comes from the Hebrew word *sedeq*, which means "the quality of being free from favoritism, self-interest, bias, or deception; especially conforming to established standards or rules."[3]

Yahweh-Elohim, the Lord God, is righteous in that He speaks and acts in accordance with the purity of His own holy nature. When God's Word declares Jesus as the King of righteousness, it is saying He is in total conformity in thought and action to the just character and nature of God, being free from any form of favoritism, self-interest, bias, or deception.

The righteousness of God is perfect justice and holiness in all things in accordance with His perfect will. Everything God does is right, just, and holy. It is impossible for God to be unjust. Everything in the kingdom of heaven is built upon righteousness and justice.

The psalmist wrote, "Righteousness and justice are the foundation of Your throne; mercy and truth go before Your face" (Ps. 89:14). At all times and in all ways Jesus is perfectly in alignment with the will of the Father. He declared this truth over and over. We must focus on the righteousness of Jesus. Being clothed with the robe of righteousness is being clothed with Jesus. This covering causes us to be hidden with Christ in God. The righteousness of God empowers us to walk as He walked.

> Set your mind on things above [on the righteousness of God], not on things on the earth. For you died, and your life is hidden with Christ in God. When Christ who is our life appears, then you also will appear with Him in glory. Therefore, put to death your members which are on the earth: fornication, uncleanness, passion, evil desire, and covetousness, which is idolatry.
>
> —COLOSSIANS 3:2–5

Jesus showed us how to live righteously on the earth.

> I can of Myself do nothing. As I hear, I judge; and
> My judgment is righteous, because I do not seek My
> own will but the will of the Father who sent Me.
>
> —JOHN 5:30

Jesus said in essence, "My judgment, My actions, My words are righteous because I do not seek My own will." As you and I focus on Jesus, hearing the still small voice of the Lord and being freed from the noise of shame, we also can walk in righteousness. The covering of the robe of righteousness gives us boldness to go to God. Our confidence is that we are robed with Jesus' righteousness, and that gives us full access to the grace and mercy of the Lord.

Again, Jesus showed us how to live out the fruit of His righteousness.

> For I have come down from heaven, not to do My
> own will, but the will of Him who sent Me. This
> is the will of the Father who sent Me, that of all
> He has given Me I should lose nothing, but should
> raise it up at the last day. And this is the will of Him
> who sent Me, that everyone who sees the Son and
> believes in Him may have everlasting life; and I will
> raise him up at the last day.
>
> —JOHN 6:38–40

It is because Jesus didn't do His own will but the will of the Father that He has the power and authority to raise us up. Jesus alone is worthy, for there is only One who was fully obedient to God. In full obedience to the Father, Jesus left His glory in heaven and came to earth as a man. He "was in all points tempted as we are, yet without sin" (Heb. 4:15). "And being found in appearance as a man, He humbled Himself and became obedient to the point of death, even the death of the cross" (Phil. 2:8).

As we discussed previously, Jesus alone was worthy to take the scroll and open the seals. As John wrote, "…for You were slain, and have redeemed us to God by Your blood out of every tribe and tongue and people and nation, and have made us kings and priests to our God; and we shall reign on the earth.…Worthy is the Lamb who was slain to receive power and riches and wisdom, and strength and honor and glory and blessing!" (Rev. 5:9–10, 12).

Jesus alone is worthy. He alone is righteous. The only way we are "made righteous" is when we remain in Him and are covered or clothed in Him. He is perfectly in line with the Father at all times, and when we are in Him we are in line with the Father as well. When the Father looks at you and me, He sees Jesus because we are *in* Him.

THE AUTHORITY OF RIGHTEOUSNESS

> But to the Son He says: "Your throne, O God, is forever and ever; a scepter of righteousness is the scepter of Your kingdom. You have loved righteousness and hated lawlessness; therefore God, Your God, has anointed You with the oil of gladness more than Your companions."
>
> —HEBREWS 1:8–9

The writer of Hebrews tells us Jesus will rule with the scepter of righteousness. A scepter speaks of authority. Jesus has all authority because He is righteous. He has all authority because He is in total conformity in thought and action to the just character and nature of God, being free from any favoritism, self-interest, bias, or deception.

Because Jesus was obedient unto death, the Father has "highly exalted Him and given Him the name which is above every name, that at the name of Jesus every knee should bow, of those in heaven, and of those on earth, and of those under the earth, and that every tongue should confess that Jesus Christ is Lord, to the glory of God the Father" (Phil. 2:9–11). Jesus is the *King of righteousness*.

WE ARE ONLY RIGHTEOUS AS WE REMAIN IN HIM

Jesus says, "Abide in Me, and I in you. As the branch cannot bear fruit of itself, unless it abides in the vine, neither can you, unless you abide in Me. I am the vine, you are the branches. He who abides in Me, and I in him, bears much fruit; for without Me you can do nothing" (John 15:4–5).

As we abide in Him, and His Word abides in us, we will be "filled with the fruits of righteousness which are by Jesus Christ" (Phil. 1:11). The fruits of righteousness manifest in our lives in direct correlation to our abiding in Him. This is why shame is such an enemy. Shame gets you focused on yourself, your failures, your weaknesses, and your reputation. Shame causes you to flee from God instead of running to Him and abiding in Him.

Shame says you are not worthy to be close to Jesus. Jesus says, "You are not worthy, so you need to abide in Me, for only I am worthy."

> In Your name they rejoice all day long, and in Your righteousness they are exalted.
>
> —Psalm 89:16

> For all have sinned and fall short of the glory of God, being justified freely by His grace through the

> redemption that is in Christ Jesus, whom God set
> forth as a propitiation [a mercy seat] by His blood,
> through faith, to demonstrate His righteousness,
> because in His forbearance God had passed over
> the sins that were previously committed, to demon-
> strate at the present time His righteousness, that He
> might be just and the justifier of the one who has
> faith in Jesus.
>
> —ROMANS 3:23–26

Jesus, by His blood, has fully paid the price for all our
sins, failures, and weaknesses. He stands before God the
Father as the King of righteousness, with all authority
having been given unto Him. When we look unto Jesus
and have faith in Him, our lives are "hidden with Christ
in God" (Col. 3:3).

God's Word instructs, "Seek those things which are
above, where Christ is, sitting at the right hand of God. Set
your mind on things above, not on things on the earth"
(Col. 3:1–2). Look unto Jesus. Focus on His righteousness.
God's Word declares, "He has clothed me with the garments of salvation; he has covered me with the robe of
righteousness" (Isa. 61:10). And Paul wrote, "For you died,
and your life is hidden with Christ in God. When Christ
who is our life appears, then you also will appear with
Him in glory" (Col. 3:3–4).

Only as we keep our eyes on Him and His righteousness, abiding in His Word, can we "come boldly to the
throne of grace, that we may obtain mercy and find grace
to help in time of need" (Heb. 4:16). And "having boldness
to enter the Holiest by the blood of Jesus…let us draw near
with a true heart in full assurance of faith, having our
hearts sprinkled from an evil conscience and our bodies

washed with pure water. Let us hold fast the confession of our hope without wavering, for He who promised is faithful" (Heb. 10:19, 22–23).

As we come boldly to God's throne, walking free from shame, we will receive power to overcome the onslaught of the enemy. He has made a way for us to access the fullness of His power as we become partakers of His divine nature.

> To those who have obtained like precious faith with us by the righteousness of our God and Savior Jesus Christ: Grace and peace be multiplied to you in the knowledge of God and of Jesus our Lord, as His divine power has given to us all things that pertain to life and godliness, through the knowledge of Him who called us by glory and virtue, by which have been given to us exceedingly great and precious promises, that through these you may be partakers of the divine nature, having escaped the corruption that is in the world through lust.
>
> —2 PETER 1:1–4

> Therefore, my beloved, as you have always obeyed… work out your own salvation with fear and trembling; for it is God who works in you both to will and to do for His good pleasure.
>
> —PHILIPPIANS 2:12–13

You were chosen before the foundation of the world to be holy and blameless before God, and you are covered with the robe of His righteousness. Say out loud, "I am *chosen*; I am *covered*." And now let's enter the revelation of "I am *crowned*."

CHAPTER 13

CROWNED WITH GLORY AND HONOR

G OD ALWAYS INTENDED for man to be crowned with glory and honor. Again, Revelation 1:5–6 says, "To Him who loved us and washed us from our sins in His own blood, and has made us kings and priests to His God and Father, to Him be glory and dominion forever and ever. Amen."

To be crowned speaks of authority, power, dominion, and majesty. We have been chosen by God to be kings and priests. As kings we have authority and dominion in the natural realm, and as priests we have authority and power in the spirit realm.

Mankind sinned and lost their ability to function in the power and authority God had bestowed upon them. God always planned for man to rule and reign with Him, but when Adam and Eve sinned mankind was disqualified. Everything in the kingdom of heaven is about authority.

When Adam and Eve violated God's commands they broke the law of love.

Jesus said, "If you love Me, keep My commandments" (John 14:15). The law of love expresses itself in obedience to God the Father. We cannot say we love God and live in disobedience to His Word. We see this again and again in Scripture.

> He who has My commandments and keeps them, it is he who loves Me. And he who loves Me will be loved by My Father, and I will love him and manifest Myself to him.
>
> —John 14:21

> Now by this we know that we know Him, if we keep His commandments. He who says, "I know Him," and does not keep His commandments, is a liar, and the truth is not in him. But whoever keeps His word, truly the love of God is perfected in him. By this we know that we are in Him. He who says he abides in Him ought himself also to walk just as He walked.
>
> —1 John 2:3–6

> Whoever believes that Jesus is the Christ is born of God, and everyone who loves Him who begot also loves him who is begotten of Him. By this we know that we love the children of God, when we love God and keep His commandments. For this is the love of God, that we keep His commandments. And His commandments are not burdensome.
>
> —1 John 5:1–3

God is "the same yesterday, today, and forever" (Heb. 13:8), and He says, "For I am the LORD, I do not change" (Mal. 3:6). The law of love never changes. If you love God, you will obey His commands. You will make a choice of your will to act in God's best interest regardless of the consequences to yourself.

When mankind sinned in the garden they violated the law of love and could no longer function as a legal representative of God's authority on the earth. Everything in the kingdom of heaven is based on authority. When Adam and Eve sinned they rejected God's authority to tell them what they could and could not do. This rejection of God's authority is the essence of all sin.

> For all have sinned and fall short of the glory of God.
> —ROMANS 3:23

> There is none righteous, no, not one.
> —ROMANS 3:10

God created mankind to be crowned with authority, glory, and honor, but we lost this in the garden. The Father then began the process of redeeming us from the law of sin and death. The wages of sin is death, but we see Jesus, "who was made a little lower than the angels, for the suffering of death crowned with glory and honor, that He, by the grace of God, might taste death for everyone" (Heb. 2:9).

Jesus paid the penalty for our disobedience by obeying the Father completely. His obedience redeemed us of our sins and bought for us the restoration of *all* things.

> Repent therefore and be converted, that your sins may be blotted out, so that times of refreshing may come from the presence of the Lord, and that He may send Jesus Christ, who was preached to you before, whom heaven must receive until the times of restoration of

all things, which God has spoken by the mouth of all
His holy prophets since the world began.

—ACTS 3:19–21

As we repent—that is, change our minds about rejecting
God's authority—and submit to God's rightful authority,
we are forgiven and brought into the kingdom of heaven.
Everything that mankind lost will be fully restored. We are
going to once again receive the crown of glory and honor.

Shame distracts us from the amazing future that awaits
us. It convinces us that we have no power, authority, or
glory. Shame, whether real or imposed upon us, causes
us to look to and judge ourselves. It convinces us we are
not royalty, have no spiritual power to overcome, and
don't have any authority. Although we lost our crown of
glory and honor through sin, Jesus through His death,
burial, and resurrection has redeemed us back to God and
restored the crown of glory and honor.

Jesus prayed, "And now, O Father, glorify Me together
with Yourself, with the glory which I had with You before
the world was....And the glory which You gave Me I have
given them" (John 17:22). And Paul wrote, "To them God
willed to make known what are the riches of the glory of
this mystery among the Gentiles: which is Christ in you,
the hope of glory" (Col. 1:27).

The glory Jesus had from the beginning with the Father
has been given to the church. This crown of glory and honor
is going to become increasingly manifest in the last days.

The prophet Isaiah declared,

Arise, shine; for your light has come! And the glory
of the LORD is risen upon you. For behold, the darkness shall cover the earth, and deep darkness the

people; but the LORD will arise over you, and His glory will be seen upon you.

—ISAIAH 60:1–2

The deepest darkness shall cover the earth when the greatest manifestation of the crown of God's glory will be seen upon the church. The greater the battles and the fiercer the attacks of the enemy, the greater the crown of glory will be seen upon us. Understanding the crown of glory upon us gives us the power to reject the lying curse of shame. You can't be filled with the revelation of the restoration of the crown of God's glory and be filled with shame at the same time. The two are polar opposites.

GLORY WHEN SUFFERING

If you are reproached for the name of Christ, blessed are you, for the Spirit of glory and of God rests upon you....Yet if anyone suffers as a Christian, let him not be ashamed, but let him glorify God in this matter.

—1 PETER 4:14, 16

The word *reproached* means to be reprimanded, reviled, mocked, and insulted for perceived faults in a harsh or demeaning manner.[1] In other words, it means to be shamed. Peter wrote that when you are reproached, or shamed, the Spirit of glory rests upon you. As the world tries to shame you the Lord will manifest the glory of God upon you more and more. This truth must become deeply embedded into our consciousness. We must see the truth that as we are under the assault of the enemy, God is revealing His glory in and through us.

Paul reveals this amazing truth in 2 Corinthians 4. He

starts by focusing on the glory of God that is inside of us as born-again believers.

> For it is the God who commanded light to shine out of darkness, who has shone in our hearts to give the light of the knowledge of the glory of God in the face of Jesus Christ.
>
> —2 CORINTHIANS 4:6

The light of the knowledge of the glory of God is revealed in the face of Jesus. Remember that as we see Him, we shall become like Him. Just a few verses earlier, Paul says in 2 Corinthians 3:18, "But we all, with unveiled face, beholding as in a mirror the glory of the Lord, are being transformed into the same image from glory to glory, just as by the Spirit of the Lord." Then in 2 Corinthians 4:7, Paul declares an incredible truth: "But we have this treasure in earthen vessels, that the excellence of the power may be of God and not of us."

This treasure of the light of the knowledge of the glory of God—this glory, this power, this fullness of God—is inside our earth vessels. But most of us do not experience much of this glory or see it manifest in and through our lives.

Paul then takes us through what I believe is one of the most overlooked truths in our modern Western gospel: the power and glory of suffering. We have the glory of God in our earthen vessels, but how is it manifested outwardly? Paul shows us.

> We are hard-pressed on every side, yet not crushed; we are perplexed, but not in despair; persecuted, but not forsaken; struck down, but not destroyed.
>
> —2 CORINTHIANS 4:8–9

> Always carrying about in the body the liability and
> exposure to the same putting to death that the Lord
> Jesus suffered, so that the [resurrection] life of Jesus
> also may be shown forth by and in our bodies.
> —2 CORINTHIANS 4:10, AMPC

> For we who live are always delivered to death for
> Jesus' sake, that the life of Jesus also may be mani-
> fested in our mortal flesh.
> —2 CORINTHIANS 4:11

As we suffer for the cause of Christ, as we are hard-pressed on every side, perplexed, persecuted, even struck down, we are not destroyed or weakened. An amazing thing starts to happen inside us. As we suffer, the resurrection life of Jesus, the glory of God, begins to manifest in and through our bodies.

Jesus wasn't just giving us comforting words when He said, "Blessed are those who are persecuted for righteousness' sake, for theirs is the kingdom of heaven" (Matt. 5:10). He was revealing a powerful truth. When you are persecuted for righteousness' sake, an authority is released into your life—a crown of glory!

Let me say that again. As we suffer for Christ, God releases and manifests a crown of glory in and through our bodies. As we suffer all manner of reviling, accusations, persecutions, and attacks, God releases a greater dimension of His authority into our lives.

This is not something we teach much in the Western churches, but throughout history this has been known. Suffering for Christ produces a glory in and through us.

> Therefore we do not lose heart. Even though our
> outward man is perishing, yet the inward man is
> being renewed day by day. For our light affliction,
> which is but for a moment, is working for us a far
> more exceeding and eternal weight of glory.
>
> —2 Corinthians 4:16–17

I love the way 2 Corinthians 4:17 reads in the Amplified
Bible, Classic Edition:

> For our light, momentary affliction (this slight dis-
> tress of the passing hour) is ever more and more
> abundantly preparing and producing and achieving
> for us an everlasting weight of glory [beyond all
> measure, excessively surpassing all comparisons
> and all calculations, a vast and transcendent glory
> and blessedness never to cease!].

Paul—who was beaten repeatedly, imprisoned, reviled,
shipwrecked, stoned, whipped, and so much more—called
these sufferings light and momentary. How could he make
such a statement? What depth of revelation did he have
that gave him such a perspective?

> We consider and look not to the things that are seen
> but to the things that are unseen; for the things
> that are visible are temporal (brief and fleeting),
> but the things that are invisible are deathless and
> everlasting.
>
> —2 Corinthians 4:18, AMPC

Paul's focus was on the eternal and spiritual, not on
the natural. He saw what God was doing through his suffering and rejoiced in it. He saw that through his sufferings for Christ, a crown of glory was being manifested. A

new dimension of the manifestation of the glory of God is revealed when God's people are suffering.

God takes what the devil means for evil and causes it to turn out for good. The apostles understood this amazing truth, and we must embrace it as well.

> My brethren, count it all joy when you fall into various trials, knowing that the testing of your faith produces patience. But let patience have its perfect work, that you may be perfect and complete, lacking nothing.
>
> —JAMES 1:2–4

> And when they had called for the apostles and beaten them, they commanded that they should not speak in the name of Jesus, and let them go. So they departed from the presence of the council, rejoicing that they were counted worthy to *suffer shame* for His name. And daily in the temple, and in every house, they did not cease teaching and preaching Jesus as the Christ.
>
> —ACTS 5:40–42, EMPHASIS ADDED

Note these specific words: "rejoicing that they were counted worthy to suffer shame for His name." Their ability to rejoice while suffering the assault of shame came from a deep revelation that the more they were attacked, the more the glory was revealed.

Paul wrote, "Therefore I take pleasure in infirmities, in reproaches, in needs, in persecutions, in distresses, for Christ's sake. For when I am weak, then I am strong" (2 Cor. 12:10). Why could Paul declare that he was strong in the midst of his trial? Because as he suffered for Christ's sake a new dimension of the crown of glory was manifesting in and through his life. The mystery of the crown of glory is for those who overcome suffering.

There is a suffering that comes when you are assaulted with shame. There is a suffering that comes when you are bombarded by the attacks of the works of the flesh. In the days we are entering into, the enemy is going to use the weapon of shame at a level never seen before. We will be able to overcome only as we understand that God uses difficult circumstances to release His glory in and through us.

Jesus despised the shame. He thought so little of it that it had no power to influence His behavior. The writer of Hebrews said, "Looking unto Jesus, the author and finisher of our faith, who for the joy that was set before Him..." (Heb. 12:2). James said, "My brethren, count it all joy when you fall into various trials" (Jas. 1:2). Paul said, "Therefore I take pleasure in infirmities, in reproaches, in needs, in persecutions, in distresses, for Christ's sake. For when I am weak, then I am strong" (2 Cor. 12:10).

There was a joy set before Jesus and the disciples that gave them the ability to overcome the shame of suffering and endure the hardships. That joy was that the glory of God would be manifest in and through them as they faithfully endured the suffering. When we look at shame we see it as a painful experience and something to be avoided. But when they looked at suffering shame for the sake of the cross they rejoiced because they knew the glory of God would rest upon them and be manifest to the world as a result.

We will be able to endure the suffering of shame when we understand that as the enemy tries to assault us with shame, the opposite thing is happening. He is trying to strike us down, but God is lifting us up. He is trying to weaken us, but the glory of the Lord will be standing up inside us. He is trying to diminish our influence, but instead the greatest manifestation of the power of God the world has ever seen will be on full display.

When we finally understand that the shame the enemy and the world heaps on us only produces a greater glory of God inside us as we focus on Him, we will think so little of being shamed that it will have no power over us. Again, we must look "unto Jesus, the author and finisher of our faith, who for the joy that was set before Him endured the cross, despising the shame, and has sat down at the right hand of the throne of God. For consider Him who endured such hostility from sinners against Himself, lest you become weary and discouraged in your souls" (Heb. 12:2–3).

CHAPTER 14

NO WEAPON FORMED AGAINST YOU SHALL PROSPER

WITH A FRESH focus on Jesus and what He is focused on, it is time to pick up our weapons of warfare and fight to defeat this enemy called shame. Jesus paid the price for our shame on the cross, but we must enforce the victory in our lives.

We need to follow Jesus' example. Hebrews 12:2 says He despised the shame. The Greek word translated "despising" in that verse means to think little of, look down on, or show contempt.[1] *Contempt* is "the feeling that a person or a thing is beneath consideration, worthless, or deserving scorn."[2] Jesus thought so little of shame that it was beneath His consideration. He was so full of the revelation knowledge of His Father and His purpose that any voice, whether internal or external, that tried to shame Him had no power to influence His behavior.

Let's go back to the Garden of Eden.

> Then the eyes of both of them were opened, and they knew that they were naked; and they sewed fig leaves together and made themselves coverings. And they heard the sound of the Lord God walking in the garden in the cool of the day, and Adam and his wife hid themselves from the presence of the Lord God among the trees of the garden. Then the Lord God called to Adam and said to him, "Where are you?"
>
> So he said, "I heard Your voice in the garden, and I was afraid because I was naked; and I hid myself." And He said, "Who told you that you were naked? Have you eaten from the tree of which I commanded you that you should not eat?"
>
> —Genesis 3:7–11

"Who told you that you were naked?" the Lord asked Adam. The Lord was focusing Adam on the truth that he was now listening to another voice. "Who told you to feel ashamed?" was the question. "What outside voice are you listening to?"

The voice of shame does not come from God. It was something man was never meant to know or experience. The voice of shame was a devastating enemy that caused Adam and Eve to hide themselves from God and refuse to take responsibility for their sins, and it ultimately got them ejected from the Garden of Eden. We all have heard the voice of shame, and we all must fight it.

Isaiah 54:17 is one of the most famous spiritual warfare

passages in Scripture. "No weapon formed against you shall prosper" is the part most people quote, but if we take a deeper look at the full context of Isaiah 54, we are going to get a revelation.

The chapter begins with,

> "Sing, O barren, you who have not borne! Break forth into singing, and cry aloud, you who have not labored with child! For more are the children of the desolate than the children of the married woman," says the LORD.
>
> "Enlarge the place of your tent, and let them stretch out the curtains of your dwellings; do not spare; lengthen your cords, and strengthen your stakes. For you shall expand to the right and to the left, and your descendants will inherit the nations, and make the desolate cities inhabited.
>
> "Do not fear, for you will not be *ashamed*; neither be disgraced, for you will not be put to *shame*; for you will forget the *shame* of your youth, and will not remember the reproach [shame] of your widowhood anymore."
>
> —ISAIAH 54:1–4, EMPHASIS ADDED

The focus of the entire chapter is on God's love and promises for His people. It tells us that God's love and promises are so great the world and the culture's attempts to shame you don't stand a chance against them. God is saying through Isaiah 54, "I have so favored you that there is no place for shame any longer in your life."

The symbol of the barren woman in Isaiah 54 is powerful. A woman who couldn't conceive was considered cursed, and she was rejected. The pain of the shame she carried was overwhelming. The prophet Samuel's mother, Hannah, wept bitterly because of her barren womb (1 Sam. 1:6–11).

Barrenness speaks of the shame of feeling worthless. Over and over in the Bible we see this play out. Now in Isaiah 54 God is saying:

> "For your Maker is your husband [the world may have rejected you, but I have made you My beloved bride], the LORD of hosts is His name [the power of the enemy cannot defeat you, for I am the Lord of the armies of heaven; you not only have My love but also My protection]; and your Redeemer is the Holy One of Israel [I am your redeemer; I am the one who has bought you back; I have redeemed you and called you by name; you are Mine and have infinite value to Me]; He is called the God of the whole earth.
>
> "For the LORD has called you like a woman forsaken and grieved in spirit, like a youthful wife when you were refused," says your God. [I chose you! When the world rejected you, I called you. I have picked you. You are *chosen*.]
>
> "For a mere moment I have forsaken you [you may have gone through terrible things and felt like I have utterly forsaken you, but those tragic seasons are but for a moment.], but with great mercies I will gather you. [My mercies endure forever. I will draw you to Myself. I will gather you from wherever you have fallen, whatever pit you're in. I will lift you up to be with Me where I am.]
>
> "With a little wrath I hid My face from you for a moment; but with everlasting kindness I will have mercy on you," says the LORD, your Redeemer. [I chose you and determined I will never leave you

nor forsake you. My kindness toward you will never cease.]

—ISAIAH 54:5–8

No matter how much we have failed, no matter how much the world has shamed us, God's mercy and kindness toward us will never cease. Look at how definitively God makes this promise in the next two verses of Isaiah 54.

"For this is like the waters of Noah to Me; for as I have sworn that the waters of Noah would no longer cover the earth, so have I sworn that I would not be angry with you, nor rebuke you. For the mountains shall depart and the hills be removed, but My kindness shall not depart from you, nor shall My covenant of peace be removed," says the LORD, who has mercy on you.

—ISAIAH 54:9–10

Heaven and earth shall pass away, but His covenant promises to His chosen will never pass away. I experienced this in an amazing way several years ago. Earlier in this book I shared the addiction battles one of my young disciples had. One day during the worst of it I chased him down and found him in a parking lot waiting for a drug buddy. When he saw me, he agreed to sit with me in my car while he waited for his buddy. It was quite cold outside. We talked for fifteen minutes or so, then his friend showed up. He jumped out of my car and said, "I'll see you later."

I knew what he was about to do. I knew he was going to get wasted again. As his friend stood outside next to him God opened my eyes. I could see both of them spiritually. I saw that his friend was filled with darkness on the inside and covered with a darkness on the outside. I knew he had never known Christ and had surrendered to deep darkness.

But then I also saw my young disciple. He was covered with darkness on the outside. I saw him in the spirit looking down at himself, and all he could see was the darkness he had surrendered to. I could tell he believed himself to be that darkness. This young man, who once had experienced a glorious salvation and deliverance but now was overcome again by drugs, believed himself to be rejected by God. He was filled with shame and had surrendered to it. But what I saw on the inside of him changed my life. I saw the most beautiful, glorious, pure white light. It was a heavenly light. I knew this young man couldn't see such a light in himself, but I saw it.

Then God spoke to me in a very authoritative and stern voice. He said, "I fight for that which is Mine." I knew that no matter how far this young man had fallen, God hadn't given up on him. Almost everyone had. Church members, friends, even family all told me to stop fighting for him. They'd say, "Just let him hit rock bottom," or, "He's made his choice." However, God said, *"I fight for that which is Mine!"*

> O you afflicted one, tossed with tempest, and not comforted.
> —ISAIAH 54:11

God promises that when you are going through the most difficult times, even if those hard times were brought on by your disobedience, "He who has begun a good work in you will complete it until the day of Jesus Christ" (Phil. 1:6). When trouble and storms surround you, when crazy viruses spread throughout the world, governments close your churches, friends disown you, the world shames you, and you feel like nothing can comfort you, God has promised a glorious future for you.

A BATTLE IN THE MIND

The battle with shame is a mental fight. If you can win the battle in the mind, nothing can keep you from walking in freedom. No weapon formed against you can prosper.

The prophet Isaiah declared,

> Behold, I will lay your stones with colorful gems,
> and lay your foundations with sapphires.
>
> —Isaiah 54:11

Even if the voice of shame is trying to tear you down, God says, "I am building you up. I will lay your foundations with sapphires." This is so powerful because sapphires are in the foundation of God's throne, as we see in the Book of Ezekiel.

> And I looked, and there in the firmament that was above the head of the cherubim, there appeared something like a sapphire stone, having the appearance of the likeness of a throne.
>
> —Ezekiel 10:1

The Lord is saying that your foundations cannot be shaken, for He has made your foundation His throne. He has "raised us up together, and made us sit together in the heavenly places in Christ Jesus, that in the ages to come He might show the exceeding riches of His grace in His kindness toward us in Christ Jesus" (Eph. 2:6–7).

Remember the promise of God's love and grace for restoration to the Laodicean church.

As many as I love, I rebuke and chasten. Therefore be zealous and repent. Behold, I stand at the door and knock. If anyone hears My voice and opens the door, I will come in to him and dine with him, and he with Me. To him who overcomes I will grant to sit with Me on My throne, as I also overcame and sat down with My Father on His throne.

—REVELATION 3:19–21

Here again God is reminding us of the crown of glory and honor He has reserved for us. Your life will not be built upon anything man can do to or say about you. God says, "You are My precious child whom I dearly love. You have ravished My heart, and I have set your feet upon a foundation that is not only a rock but is beautiful, glorious, and established in My righteousness."

When you look unto Jesus, when you see Him as He is, you will begin to understand who you really are. God has set your feet upon the foundation of His throne, and His throne will endure forever.

Isaiah went on to say:

I will make your pinnacles of rubies.

—ISAIAH 54:12

Pinnacles are fortifications, the battlements that protect you during an assault. God says He will make them of rubies. Rubies are second in hardness to diamonds. They are bright red, which speaks of the blood of Jesus. And in Proverbs 8:11 God connects rubies with wisdom, saying "wisdom is better than rubies." So in Isaiah 54:12 God is telling us, "I will form the fortifications of your mind with My wisdom, which is rooted in the revelation of the blood of Jesus."

Nothing will be able to cross the boundary of the blood to penetrate your mind. The blood not only cleanses you of your sin; it protects you from the enemy. Death cannot cross the blood of Jesus applied to the doorway of your heart.

Your gates of crystal...

—Isaiah 54:12

Speaking of the doorway of your heart, the Bible uses gates constantly in reference to the access point to a fortified area. The image in verses 12 and 13 of Isaiah 54 are of a fortified city; however, they speak symbolically of us individually and as the church universal.

I love that Isaiah writes that the entrance to your heart will be crystal. Crystal gives the sense of complete purity as well as being incredibly hard. God is saying, "I will make the entrance to your heart pure, holy, transparent, and unbreakable. It will be a tender heart toward Me, a heart of holiness, and yet unable to be polluted by the world."

The Lord said through the prophet Ezekiel:

I will give you a new heart and put a new spirit within you; I will take the heart of stone out of your flesh and give you a heart of flesh. I will put My Spirit within you and cause you to walk in My statutes, and you will keep My judgments and do them....I will deliver you from all your uncleanness.

—EZEKIEL 36:26–27, 29

We go on to read in Isaiah 54:12,

And all your walls of precious stones.

God is saying, "I will adorn you with the beauty of holiness, humility, wisdom, and love. Out of your affliction and torment, I will perfect you." This is why James 1:2–4 tells us, "My brethren, count it all joy when you fall into various trials, knowing that the testing of your faith produces patience. But let patience have its perfect work, that you may be perfect and complete, lacking nothing."

Isaiah 54 continues with verse 13:

> All your children shall be taught by the Lord, and
> great shall be the peace of your children.

This verse is saying that through the battles and attacks of the enemy, God will fill you with the revelation knowledge of Him. You will see Him as He is, and then you will "know and understand the hope to which He has called you, and how rich is His glorious inheritance in the saints (His set-apart ones), and [so that you can know and understand] what is the immeasurable and unlimited and surpassing greatness of His power in and for us who believe, as demonstrated in the working of His mighty strength" (Eph. 1:18–19, AMPC).

The key themes of *Satan's Big Fat Lie* are all in Isaiah 54:

- the declaration that we will be delivered from our shame

- the focus on the truth that we are chosen by God

- the proclamation that we are covered in His righteousness

- the promise of being crowned with glory and honor

> In righteousness you shall be established; you shall
> be far from oppression, for you shall not fear; and
> from terror, for it shall not come near you.
>
> —ISAIAH 54:14

He will establish you in righteousness, which will result
in you being far from oppression. If Satan cannot cause
you to be filled with shame, he cannot cause you to be
oppressed. You won't be afraid like Adam was and run
from God, but you will go boldly to the throne of grace to
receive mercy and find grace to help in your time of need.
When you walk in the revelation that you are chosen, covered, and crowned, death no longer has any terror for you.
It won't matter what people try to do to you or how they
try to shame you; they can't win.

Isaiah then tells us that though you will battle shame,
the shame did not come from God.

> Indeed they shall surely assemble, *but not because
> of Me*. Whoever assembles against you shall fall for
> your sake.
>
> —ISAIAH 54:15, EMPHASIS ADDED

Battles will come. False accusers will rise up. The culture, governments, religious institutions, evil men, and
even friends and family may turn on you, accuse you, and
attack you, but in the end they shall all fall. There is no
power in heaven or earth that God Himself did not create
and does not have total power over.

Isaiah 54 continues,

> Behold, I have created the blacksmith who blows
> the coals in the fire, who brings forth an instru-
> ment for his work; and I have created the spoiler to
> destroy.
>
> —ISAIAH 54:16

Now, in the context of the battle with shame, God tells us to pick up our weapons and fight. This leads us to a verse that is so familiar.

> No weapon formed against you shall prosper, and
> every tongue which rises against you in judgment,
> you shall condemn.
>
> —ISAIAH 54:17

We love to say, "No weapon formed against you shall prosper." But often we apply it broadly. As I said previously, in context it is more specifically dealing with the voices of shame.

God asked Adam, "Who told you that you were naked?" Here, in Isaiah 54:17, we see God saying, "Every tongue which rises against you in judgment you shall condemn." In other words, every voice that rises up to shame or condemn you shall not prosper against you.

Any voice that rises up to place a judgment on you other than what God has said will no longer have any power over you. He says you shall condemn it. You shall speak to those lies and defeat them. The word *condemn* in this verse means you will declare those words guilty of wickedness.[3] You will declare them illegal. Because we now are walking in the revelation of who Jesus is and that we are chosen, covered, and crowned, we have power and authority over every voice of shame.

> "This is the heritage of the servants of the LORD, and
> their righteousness is from Me," says the LORD.
> —ISAIAH 54:17

Here at the end of this amazing prophetic chapter God establishes the fact that we are covered in His righteousness. He concludes everything He says about the attacks of shame, judgment, and accusations by telling us that we, His people, have an amazing heritage. We have the power and authority to condemn every voice of shame because our righteousness comes from Him.

You have the legal right to condemn—to declare evil and illegal—every voice of shame because you have the righteousness of God. You are chosen, you are covered, you are crowned, and as a result you can exercise the authority you have been given *when you obey.*

Jesus said,

> I will give you the keys of the kingdom of heaven;
> and whatever you bind (declare to be improper and
> unlawful) on earth must be what is already bound
> in heaven; and whatever you loose (declare lawful)
> on earth must be what is already loosed in heaven.
> —MATTHEW 16:19, AMPC

Our authority comes from knowing and obeying God's Word. God has made available to us incredible spiritual weapons to win the battle against shame. But we are weak and vulnerable when we don't know Him.

> So Jesus said to those Jews who had believed in Him,
> If you abide in My word [hold fast to My teachings
> and live in accordance with them], you are truly My

disciples. And you will know the Truth, and the Truth will set you free.

—JOHN 8:31–32, AMPC

As we abide in His Word and in the revelation of who He is, we are set free. If the enemy can't defeat you with shame, he can't drive you to hide from God when you sense His presence. Everything is exposed in the light of God's presence. We will either run to Him or from Him.

Shame was the first manifestation of sin in the garden and the last enemy Jesus defeated on the cross to fulfill His destiny and destroy the power of death once and for all. It is not enough to simply believe we are the righteousness of God; we must pick up the weapon of that revelation and use it.

WAGING WAR AGAINST SHAME

Second Corinthians 10:3–5 is another famous spiritual warfare passage, but let's look at it closely in the Amplified Bible, Classic Edition. These verses are loaded with revelation.

> For though we walk (live) in the flesh, we are not carrying on our warfare according to the flesh and using mere human weapons. For the weapons of our warfare are not physical [weapons of flesh and blood], but they are mighty before God for the overthrow and destruction of strongholds, [inasmuch as we] refute arguments and theories and reasonings and every proud and lofty thing that sets itself up against the [true] knowledge of God; and we lead every thought and purpose away captive into the obedience of Christ (the Messiah, the Anointed One).

You can't use human tactics to defeat this enemy of shame. You can't shame the people who are trying to shame you. This is a grave error and trick of the enemy. I see this all the time. There are many in the church who have embraced hyper-grace teaching. When someone comes along and presents holy living to them, they accuse them of being legalistic and religious.

Pastors from around the world have told me they can't even correct unmarried young couples in their church who are sleeping together. When the pastor addresses their sin, they accuse him of preaching the law and bondage. They claim that Jesus' blood paid the price, so it doesn't matter how they live. They call those pastors religious. In other words, they are saying, "Pastor, shame on you for confronting our sin. Shame on you; you're not loving. Shame on you; you are a preacher of bondage and are actually rejecting the cross of Christ."

Of course, these accusations are all false but very effective, because many pastors themselves are not living free from the power of shame. These young people in sin grab false doctrines and the weapon of shame to try to cover their own shame. Far too often the pastors yield to the threats of shame and stay quiet because they don't want to be accused of being legalistic, religious, and unloving. Some even begin to compromise the message to be accepted and avoid the shame of being called a holiness preacher.

Both the couples in sin and the pastors who cower to them are using the weapons of the enemy—they are shaming others, compromising, being cowardly, and denying the truth to try to defeat the spirit of shame. Again, Paul says, "For the weapons of our warfare are not physical [weapons of flesh and blood], but they are mighty before God for the overthrow and destruction of strongholds" (2 Cor. 10:4, AMPC). We cannot fight against shame using natural weapons. We must use the spiritual weapons God has given us.

We must refute every argument, theory, reasoning, and false teaching that stands in the way of the true knowledge of who Jesus really is (2 Cor. 10:5). The enemy only wins when we remain spiritually ignorant. This is why God gave us thirty amazing descriptions of Jesus in the first three chapters of the Book of Revelation and over one hundred descriptions across the whole book. God was preparing an end-time generation for the most intense battles man will ever face. The true revelation knowledge of God is the spiritual weapon we need to defeat the enemy.

Paul then tells us what we must do. Again, 2 Corinthians 10:5 (AMPC) says, "We lead every thought and purpose away captive into the obedience of Christ (the Messiah, the Anointed One)." We must be aggressive and take every thought captive and make it obey Christ. We must pick up the Word of God and speak to those thoughts of shame. It is not good enough to simply say internally, "I don't accept this." You must go on the offense and speak to those lies.

This truth is well established in Scripture and is going to be more needed in these last days than at any time in history. Joshua 1:8–9 says:

> This Book of the Law shall not depart from your mouth, but you shall meditate in it day and night, that you may observe to do according to all that is written in it. For then you will make your way prosperous, and then you will have good success. Have I not commanded you? Be strong and of good

courage; do not be afraid, nor be dismayed, for the
LORD your God is with you wherever you go.

The word translated "meditate" in Joshua 1:8 means to
mutter or speak under your breath.[4] You must speak the
words of the revelation of Jesus day and night. Declare
continually who Jesus is. God told Moses to command the
children of Israel to constantly speak His words.

> Hear, O Israel: The LORD our God, the LORD is one!
> You shall love the LORD your God with all your heart,
> with all your soul, and with all your strength. And
> these words which I command you today shall be in
> your heart. You shall teach them diligently to your
> children, and shall talk of them when you sit in your
> house, when you walk by the way, when you lie down,
> and when you rise up. You shall bind them as a sign
> on your hand, and they shall be as frontlets between
> your eyes. You shall write them on the doorposts of
> your house and on your gates.
> —DEUTERONOMY 6:4–9

God commanded the Israelites to constantly *teach His
Word*, especially to their children. He told them to *talk
about His Word* in every situation and at all times. He
instructed them to *bind the Word to themselves*—in other
words, they should publicly identify with the Word and
the God of Israel and not with the heathen nations. And
finally He told them to *write the Word*.

These four steps are to be repeated continually. Teaching,
talking, identifying with, and writing the Word causes it
to be written upon your heart. What is written upon your
heart will become your nature. If God's Word is written
on your heart, you will do by nature what the Word

commands. Your mind will be aligned with the mind of Christ, and you too will be able to endure your cross, despising the shame. And "no weapon formed against you shall prosper and every tongue that rises up in judgment [shame] you shall condemn" (Isa. 54:17).

CHAPTER 15

HIS MERCY ENDURES FOREVER

THE WARNING I received from the Lord in the vision I shared in chapter 1 was profound. He showed me an unprecedented battle that was coming in the days ahead. The enemy will unleash an onslaught of the works of the flesh unlike anything we have ever seen before. Nobody will escape being hit by this, and many will be overcome for a season.

The attacks of shame will be like a swarm of screaming crows that will try to rob God's people of their spiritual vision. These shame attacks will be the final weapon the enemy uses to try to defeat and destroy the army of God. We all must fight this together for one another.

We are all going to get hit. We are all going to battle shame, whether because of our actual sins, sins we are accused of, our associations, or false attacks from the world. We all must recognize that shame is not from God. We must stand up together and give no place to shame.

When our brothers and sisters fall, we who are spiritual must restore them. When our brothers and sisters are falsely accused, we must stand with them, even if we are accused also. When the world shames members of the body of Christ for standing for truth, we must be willing to suffer with them.

Jesus gives us the one final key for walking in victory through this onslaught of the enemy. He declares it in the Sermon on the Mount:

> Blessed are the merciful: for they shall obtain mercy.
> —Matthew 5:7

I remember a season in my church in Corona, California, when we had been in revival for nine months. Our little church had seen over a thousand youth saved in just a few months through our street evangelism. We were having services five nights a week, and the manifestation of God's presence was powerful.

We were at the end of forty days of prayer and fasting, and there was a strong spirit of prayer and consecration upon the whole church. Even the newest believers were praying multiple hours every day. I wasn't watching any TV or anything that could pass as entertainment. I spent five-plus hours a day in prayer and engaged in much fasting. It was probably the most consecrated season of my life.

On the final night of the revival I was sitting on the steps of the platform getting ready to dismiss when I just fell backward under a powerful presence of God. I lay there for about thirty minutes and couldn't move. About ten minutes after I fell back, one of the elders came and prayed over me by grabbing my feet.

Ten minutes later I felt another set of hands grab my feet. At first the hold was soft, but then the grip became quite firm. As the second set of hands gripped my feet firmly, I started to shake under the mighty power of God.

The hands released, and a few moments later I was able to open my eyes. I later asked who the second person was who prayed for me, but everyone insisted that no one was praying for me while I was shaking. I knew then that it must have been an angel.

When I sat up the Lord spoke to me. He said, "Son, during this season you have never lived holier and more separated unto Me. Yet even in this season, your sin is worthy of eternal damnation." I was shocked by those words, but I knew them to be true, for "there is none righteous, no, not one" (Rom. 3:10).

As the Lord spoke this to me, talking with me as if we were face to face, I heard a second voice of the Lord speak. This second one was loud and booming, like something you'd hear in a huge echo chamber. The second voice of the Lord thundered, saying, "But My mercy endures forever." I knew in that moment that if God's mercy were ever to stop even for a moment, I would be lost forever. But praise be to God, His mercy endures forever.

This simple but powerful experience has greatly affected my life. I will always preach a radical surrender to God and a continual pursuit of holiness. At the same time I also understand that we all fall short of the glory of God, and without God's mercy we would be lost.

A wonderful balance between preaching the holiness of God and walking in the mercy of God is expressed in

Proverbs 16:6, "By mercy and truth iniquity is purged: and by the fear of the Lord men depart from evil." The iniquity in our lives is removed by the application of both mercy and truth. It is never just one or the other. As we fix our eyes on Jesus, we must see Him as the King of righteousness, full of mercy and truth.

"Mercy and truth have met together; righteousness and peace have kissed" (Ps. 85:10). "For we do not have a High Priest who cannot sympathize with our weaknesses, but was in all points tempted as we are, yet without sin. Let us therefore come boldly to the throne of grace, that we may obtain mercy and find grace to help in time of need" (Heb. 4:15–16).

As we look unto Jesus and see Him as He is, we need not fear being exposed by truth, for the God who is the truth is also the God of everlasting mercy. Adam and Eve hid themselves because their eyes were on the shame of their sin and not on the God of mercy and truth. The voices of shame kept them from being able to see God as He is.

The voices of shame will always be screaming. We, however, have a hope: the helmet of the hope of salvation that cancels the noise of the shame and the battle. It is a helmet that enables us to hear the still, small voice of the Lord and fills our minds with perfect peace.

As we march forward in the days ahead, we must keep our eyes on Jesus. We also must be the ambassadors of reconciliation for our brothers and sisters who have fallen. With love and compassion, we must help them rise back up and teach them to pick up their weapons, regain their spiritual eyesight, put on their helmets, and get focused on Jesus and what He is focused on.

We must determine in our hearts to leave no one behind.

No matter how much someone has failed, sinned, stumbled, or even denied the Lord, there is reconciliation for the repentant. As we love them, care for them, point them to get their eyes back on Jesus, and lead them in the ways of righteousness, they too can begin to defeat the curse of shame.

Paul instructs us to walk in forgiveness.

> Now whom you forgive anything, I also forgive. For if indeed I have forgiven anything, I have forgiven that one for your sakes in the presence of Christ, lest Satan should take advantage of us; for we are not ignorant of his devices.
>
> —2 CORINTHIANS 2:10–11

If we forgive quickly as Christ forgives, then shame from the enemy can't take root in the hearts of God's people. Blessed are the merciful for they shall obtain mercy.

Revelation 4:3 describes God's throne as being surrounded by a rainbow. The rainbow is God's symbol of everlasting mercy. God's throne is surrounded on all sides by mercy. Everyone who approaches God must pass through His mercy, and everything that proceeds from God passes through His mercy. Everything God does is done through His mercy.

Jesus said in John 15:5, "I am the vine; you are the branches. Whoever abides in me and I in him, he it is that bears much fruit, for apart from me you can do nothing" (ESV). Only as we keep looking unto Jesus and focus on what He is focused on can we overcome. It is not by our might, nor by our power, but by His Spirit that any of us can defeat the curse of shame. We overcome shame only because God, in His gracious mercy, sent His Son Jesus to pay the price for all our sin and conquer the power of death, hell, and the grave once and for all.

FIX YOUR EYES ON JESUS

Again, Hebrews 12:2 says,

> Looking unto Jesus, the author and finisher of our faith, who for the joy that was set before Him endured the cross, despising the shame, and has sat down at the right hand of the throne of God.

I like the way the New Living Translation puts it:

> Therefore, since we are surrounded by such a huge crowd of witnesses to the life of faith, let us strip off every weight that slows us down, especially the sin that so easily trips us up. And let us run with endurance the race God has set before us. We do this by keeping our eyes on Jesus, the champion who initiates and perfects our faith. *Because of the joy* awaiting him, he endured the cross, disregarding its shame. Now he is seated in the place of honor beside God's throne.
>
> —HEBREWS 12:1–2, EMPHASIS ADDED

The Greek word translated "looking" in Hebrews 12:1 is *aphoraō*. It means "to turn the eyes away from other things and fix them on something."[1] The English word *look* means "to direct your eyes in a particular direction";[2] it is to fix attention on, fix our eyes, or learn about; to look away from all else. Looking unto Jesus means actively and continually looking away from all else and fixing our attention, our eyes, upon Him to learn about Him.

The revelation knowledge of God transforms the human

heart unlike anything else under grace, including miracles, experiences with God's power, answers to prayer, or divine intervention in our circumstances. The revelation knowledge of God comes only from actively fixing our attention on Him for the purpose of knowing and understanding Him, worshipping Him, and being changed into His image.

The knowledge of who we are in Christ is no match for the transforming power of seeing Jesus as He is. What He does for us cannot compare to *who He is*. This is why so many people receive a touch from God but still struggle in their faith, with some even walking away from God. Even though they felt His hand on their lives, they failed to see Him as He is. If we are truly going to see Jesus as He is, we must do it with all our hearts. This is not something that is casually done. You're not going to receive this by carving out a few minutes to read a scripture and send up a brief prayer. We are going to have to meditate on the Word day and night (Josh. 1:8; Ps. 1:2).

> And from the days of John the Baptist until the present time, the kingdom of heaven has endured violent assault, and violent men seize it by force [as a precious prize—a share in the heavenly kingdom is sought with most ardent zeal and intense exertion].
> —MATTHEW 11:12, AMPC

God has declared that "the secret things belong to the Lord our God, but those things which are revealed belong to us" (Deut. 29:29). You will receive the things of God and walk in His fullness only to the degree that you have the revelation knowledge of God.

As I mentioned previously, one great truth I have

learned in my decades of walking with the Lord is to pray and declare the Word of God. So as we come to the close of this book, this is my prayer and declaration over you:

> *"[For I always pray to] the God of our Lord Jesus Christ, the Father of glory, that He may grant you a spirit of wisdom and revelation [of insight into mysteries and secrets] in the [deep and intimate] knowledge of Him"* (Eph. 1:17, AMPC). *I pray that you will seek Him and find Him when you search for Him with all your heart* (Jer. 29:13). *"It is the glory of God to conceal a matter, but the glory of kings is to search out a matter"* (Prov. 25:2). *"To you it has been given to know the mysteries of the kingdom of God"* (Luke 8:10). *"...by having the eyes of your heart flooded with light, so that you can know and understand the hope to which He has called you, and how rich is His glorious inheritance in the saints"* (Eph. 1:18, AMPC).
>
> *"For it is the God who commanded light to shine out of darkness, who has shone in our hearts to give the light of the knowledge of the glory of God in the face of Jesus Christ"* (2 Cor. 4:6). *Because we "continued to behold [in the Word of God] as in a mirror the glory of the Lord," we "are constantly being transfigured into His very own image in ever increasing splendor and from one degree of glory to another; [for this comes] from the Lord [Who is] the Spirit"* (2 Cor. 3:18, AMPC).

For *"'eye has not seen, nor ear heard, nor have entered into the heart of man the things which God has prepared for those who love Him.' But God has revealed them to us through His Spirit. For the Spirit searches all things, yes, the deep things of God"* (1 Cor. 2:9–10).

"When He, the Spirit of truth, has come, He will guide you into all truth" (John 16:13). *"And you shall know the truth, and the truth shall make you free"* (John 8:32), *"[so that you can know and understand] what is the immeasurable and unlimited and surpassing greatness of His power in and for us who believe"* (Eph. 1:19, AMPC). *Amen.*

NOTES

CHAPTER 2

1. James Swanson, *Dictionary of Biblical Languages With Semantic Domains: Hebrew (Old Testament)* (Oak Harbor, WA: Faithlife, 1997), Logos edition.
2. Bible Sense Lexicon, s.v. *"euperistatos,"* Logos Bible Software.
3. Oxford Languages, s.v. "shame," accessed December 5, 2021, https://www.google.com/search?client=safari&rls=en&q=shame+definition&ie=UTF-8&oe=UTF-8.

CHAPTER 3

1. Swanson, *Dictionary of Biblical Languages With Semantic Domains: Hebrew (Old Testament)*.
2. "Archaeologists Identify Traces of 'Miracle' Pool," Associated Press, December 23, 2004, https://www.nbcnews.com/id/wbna6750670.
3. Blue Letter Bible, s.v. *"xērainō,"* accessed December 13, 2021, https://www.blueletterbible.org/lexicon/g3583/kjv/tr/0-1/.
4. Charles Finney, *Lectures on Systematic Theology* (Oberlin, OH: J. M. Finch, 1846), 256.
5. Charles G. Finney, *Lectures to Professing Christians, Third Edition* (London: Thomas Tegg, 1839), 134.
6. Charles Finney, "Lecture V. The Law of God," *The Oberlin Evangelist,* 1, no. 6 (February 27, 1839): 41–42, http://dcollections.oberlin.edu/digital/collection/evangelist/id/6155/rec/61.
7. Blue Letter Bible, s.v. *"rûaḥ,"* accessed January 14, 2022, https://www.blueletterbible.org/lexicon/h7307/kjv/wlc/0-1/.

CHAPTER 5

1. Oxford Languages, s.v. "shame."

CHAPTER 6

1. Grafted, "Episode 6 of Season 2 was POWERFUL!" YouTube, June 24, 2021, https://www.youtube.com/watch?v=szkCjaOQuv8, time stamp, 16:15 and 24:09.
2. Grafted, "Episode 6 of Season 2 was POWERFUL!"
3. David Pawson, *Simon Peter: The Reed and the Rock* (Ashford, UK: Anchor Recordings, 2013).

CHAPTER 7

1. "1980 Democratic Party Platform," The American Presidency Project, accessed December 15, 2021, https://www.presidency.ucsb.edu/documents/1980-democratic-party-platform.
2. Nicole Kobie, "The Complicated Truth About China's Social Credit System," *Wired*, July 6, 2019, https://www.wired.co.uk/article/china-social-credit-system-explained.

CHAPTER 8

1. *Encyclopaedia Britannica*, s.v. "Domitian," accessed December 16, 2021, https://www.britannica.com/biography/Domitian.
2. Megan Sauter, "The Church of Laodicea in the Bible and Archaeology," Biblical Archaeology Society, December 25, 2021, biblicalarchaeology.org/daily/biblical-sites-places/biblical-archaeology-sites/church-of-laodicea-in-the-bible-and-archaeology/.
3. Mike Bickle, "Knowing God: The Glory of Jesus as the Son of Man (Rev. 1-3)," The Mike Bickle Library, accessed February 1, 2022, https://backup.storage.sardius.media/file/akamaiBackup-ihopkc-103762/IHOP/718/695/20120421_Knowing_God_Glory_of_Jesus_as_the_Son_of_Man_PFJ02.pdf.
4. *Encyclopaedia Britannica*, s.v. "Black Death," accessed December 16, 2021, https://www.britannica.com/event/Black-Death/Effects-and-significance.
5. "WHO Coronavirus (COVID-19) Dashboard," World Health Organization, December 16, 2021, https://covid19.who.int/.

6. "World Population Dashboard," United Nations Population Fund, accessed December 16, 2021, https://www.unfpa.org/data/world-population-dashboard.
7. "Day 6—Colossae, Laodicea, and Hierapolis," GTI Study Tours, October 16, 2012, https://archive.gtitours.org/journals/2012-10-09-israel-turkey-tour/day-6-colossae-laodicea-and-hierapolis/.

CHAPTER 11

1. *Merriam-Webster*, s.v. "ravish," accessed December 19, 2021, https://www.merriam-webster.com/dictionary/ravished.
2. Oxford Languages, s.v. "ravish," accessed December 18, 2021, https://www.google.com/search?q=definition+of+ravished.
3. Isaac Bennett, "The Delight of Christ: Preparing for Testing—Song. 4," Forerunner Church, accessed December 19, 2021, https://static1.squarespace.com/static/5acdc7203e2d09e44729613f/t/6187e128725fb64f5c11cd42/1636294952975/The+Delight+of+Christ+-+Preparing+for+Testing+-+Song+4.pdf.

CHAPTER 12

1. Blue Letter Bible, s.v. "*dikaios*," accessed December 19, 2021, https://www.blueletterbible.org/lexicon/g1342/kjv/tr/0-1/.
2. Swanson, *Dictionary of Biblical Languages With Semantic Domains: Hebrew (Old Testament)*.
3. Exegetical Guide (Logos Bible Software), s.v. "*sedeq*."

CHAPTER 13

1. Exegetical Guide (Logos Bible Software), s.v. "1 Peter 4:14–16."

CHAPTER 14

1. Blue Letter Bible, s.v. "*kataphroneō*," accessed December 2, 2021, https://www.blueletterbible.org/lexicon/g2706/kjv/tr/0-1/.
2. Lexico, s.v. "contempt," accessed January 27, 2022, https://www.lexico.com/en/definition/contempt.

3. Blue Letter Bible, s.v. "*rāša‘*," accessed December 20, 2021, https://www.blueletterbible.org/lexicon/h7561/kjv/wlc/0-1/.
4. Blue Letter Bible, s.v. "*hāḡâ*," accessed December 20, 2021, https://www.blueletterbible.org/lexicon/h1897/kjv/wlc/0-1/.

CHAPTER 15

1. Blue Letter Bible, s.v. "*aphoraō*," accessed December 17, 2021, https://www.blueletterbible.org/lexicon/g872/kjv/tr/0-1/.
2. *Merriam-Webster*, s.v. "look," accessed January 14, 2022, https://www.merriam-webster.com/dictionary/looking.